D1529043

SWITZERLAND TRAVEL GUIDE

The Most Updated Pocket Guide to the
Land of Chocolate | Discover Switzerland's
History, Art, Culture, Landscapes and
Hidden Gems to Plan an Unforgettable Trip

By

DANIEL N. MARTIN

Table of Contents

1

Introduction

Switzerland, nestled in the heart of Europe, is a country renowned for its breathtaking natural landscapes, enchanting cities, and rich cultural heritage. With its snow-capped mountains, pristine lakes, charming villages, and efficient public transportation system, Switzerland has long been a dream destination for travelers seeking both adventure and tranquility.

The country's official languages are German, French, Italian, and Romansh, reflecting its diverse cultural influences. This linguistic diversity adds to the country's allure, as each region has its own unique character and attractions.

Switzerland is perhaps best known for its majestic Alps, which dominate the southern part of the country. Here, adventure seekers can indulge in a myriad of activities, including skiing, snowboarding, hiking, and mountaineering. Famous mountain resorts like Zermatt, St. Moritz, and Verbier offer world-class facilities and stunning vistas that attract visitors from all over the globe.

Aside from its mountains, Switzerland boasts an extensive network of shimmering lakes. The iconic Lake Geneva, located in the west, offers a picturesque setting with the stunning backdrop of the Alps. The charming cities that surround the lake, such as Geneva, Lausanne, and Montreux, are filled with historical landmarks, vibrant cultural scenes, and delicious cuisine.

Travelers to Switzerland will also find themselves captivated by the medieval old towns and charming villages dotted throughout the country. Cities like Zurich, Bern, and Lucerne blend modernity with history, boasting beautifully preserved architecture, museums, and bustling marketplaces. Meanwhile, smaller towns like Gruyères, Interlaken, and Zermatt exude an idyllic charm, inviting visitors to wander their narrow streets and immerse themselves in Swiss traditions.

One of Switzerland's greatest assets is its world-class transportation system, known for its efficiency, punctuality, and stunning scenic routes. The Swiss Travel Pass provides unlimited access to trains, buses, and boats, making it easy to explore the country's diverse regions. Traveling by train through the picturesque landscapes is an experience in itself, with panoramic windows offering breathtaking views of mountains, lakes, and rolling meadows. Switzerland is also renowned for its culinary delights. From Swiss chocolates and cheeses to delicious fondue and raclette, the country offers a tantalizing array of flavors that will satisfy even the most discerning palate. Be sure to indulge in local specialties and explore the vibrant food scenes in various cities and towns.

While Switzerland is an all-season destination, each time of year offers a different experience. Winter is ideal for skiing and snowboarding enthusiasts, while spring and summer provide opportunities for hiking, cycling, and exploring the countryside. Autumn paints the landscape in vibrant colors, and many festivals and events take place throughout the year, showcasing the country's traditions and cultural heritage.

In this comprehensive Switzerland travel guide, we will delve deeper into the country's regions, cities, attractions, activities, and practical information to help you plan your dream trip. Whether you seek adventure in the mountains, cultural immersion in historic cities, or simply wish to bask in Switzerland's natural beauty, this guide will be your ultimate companion in discovering the best of Switzerland. So pack your bags, prepare your camera, and get ready for an unforgettable journey through this alpine paradise.

Chapter 1.
The historical overview
of Switzerland.

The history of Switzerland is a fascinating tapestry woven with tales of independence, cultural diversity, and political neutrality. The region that comprises modern-day Switzerland has been inhabited for thousands of years, with evidence of human presence dating back to the Paleolithic era. Here is a detailed historical overview of Switzerland, highlighting key periods and events:

1. Ancient Times:

- Prehistoric Swiss tribes, such as the Helvetians, inhabited the region before the Roman conquest.
- In 15 BC, the Romans established the province of Raetia, which covered parts of present-day Switzerland.
- Roman influence brought infrastructure, urbanization, and the spread of Christianity.

2. Medieval Era:

    •   During the early Middle Ages, the territory that would become Switzerland was fragmented into numerous feudal domains.

    •   The rise of powerful families and cities led to increased autonomy and the formation of cantons (self-governing regions).

    •   The three original Swiss cantons, Uri, Schwyz, and Unterwalden, formed a defensive alliance in 1291, known as the Swiss Confederation.

3. Expansion of the Swiss Confederation:

    •   The Swiss Confederation gradually expanded as more cantons joined the alliance.

    •   The Battle of Morgarten in 1315 marked a significant victory for the Confederation against the Habsburgs, solidifying their independence.

    •   By the 16th century, there were 13 cantons in the Confederation.

4. Reformation and Religious Conflicts:

    •   The Protestant Reformation, led by figures like Huldrych Zwingli and John Calvin, gained momentum in Switzerland during the 16th century.

    •   The religious divide between Protestant and Catholic cantons led to internal conflicts and religious wars, such as the Kappel Wars.

    •   The Peace of Westphalia in 1648 recognized Switzerland as an independent nation within the Holy Roman Empire.

5. Napoleonic Era and Swiss Federal State:

- In 1798, French revolutionary forces invaded Switzerland, leading to the collapse of the Old Swiss Confederation.

- The Helvetic Republic, a centralized state inspired by French revolutionary ideals, was established.

- Napoleon's campaigns and subsequent Congress of Vienna (1815) shaped the modern boundaries of Switzerland.

- In 1848, Switzerland adopted a new federal constitution, establishing the Swiss Federal State.

6. Neutrality and International Relations:

   - Switzerland has maintained a policy of neutrality since the Congress of Vienna, avoiding involvement in international conflicts.

   - The Swiss Confederation has acted as a mediator in numerous international disputes and hosted diplomatic negotiations.

   - Switzerland remained neutral during both World Wars, although it faced challenges in maintaining its sovereignty and economy.

7. Modern Switzerland:

   - In the 20th century, Switzerland experienced significant social, economic, and political changes.
   - Women gained suffrage in 1971, and the country became more ethnically diverse through immigration.
   - Switzerland is not a member of the European Union but maintains close ties and agreements through bilateral agreements.

Today, Switzerland is a prosperous and politically stable country known for its direct democracy, high standard of living, and international organizations headquartered in Geneva. Its historical legacy is celebrated through preserved medieval towns, museums, and cultural traditions that reflect the nation's unique blend of German, French, Italian, and Romansh influences.

Cultural heritage art and architecture

Switzerland's cultural heritage is a testament to its rich history, diverse influences, and artistic traditions. From ancient Roman ruins to medieval castles, from Renaissance masterpieces to contemporary architectural marvels, Switzerland offers a wealth of cultural treasures. Here is an in-depth exploration of the country's cultural heritage, art, and architecture:

1. Architecture:

Traditional Swiss Architecture: The country is known for its distinctive traditional architecture, characterized by wooden chalets with steeply sloping roofs, intricate woodwork, and decorative facades. These charming chalets can be found in alpine villages and mountain regions.

Romanesque and Gothic Architecture: Romanesque and Gothic styles left their mark on Switzerland's religious buildings, such as cathedrals, churches, and monasteries. Notable examples include the Grossmünster and Fraumünster churches in Zurich, as well as the Cathedral of Lausanne.

Renaissance and Baroque Architecture: Renaissance and Baroque influences can be seen in palaces, town halls, and aristocratic residences. The Palace of Parliament in Bern and the Château de Chillon on Lake Geneva are prominent examples.

Modern and Contemporary Architecture: Switzerland embraces modern and contemporary architecture, with notable architects like Le Corbusier and Mario Botta having left their mark. The Kunsthaus Zürich, the Vitra Design Museum, and the Rolex Learning Center are striking examples of modern architectural achievements.

2. Art:

Swiss Folk Art: Switzerland has a strong tradition of folk art, which encompasses various forms such as woodcarving, embroidery, pottery, and textile arts. These traditional crafts often reflect regional styles and motifs.

Medieval and Renaissance Art: The influence of medieval and Renaissance art can be seen in religious paintings, sculptures, and illuminated manuscripts found in churches and museums across the country. The Museums of Fine Arts in Zurich and Basel house impressive collections.

Symbolism and Expressionism: In the late 19th and early 20th centuries, Swiss artists embraced Symbolism and Expressionism, exploring themes of spirituality, mythology, and the human condition. Artists like Ferdinand Hodler and Cuno Amiet made significant contributions to these movements.

Contemporary Art: Switzerland has a vibrant contemporary art scene, with numerous galleries, art festivals, and museums showcasing the works of both Swiss and international artists. The Kunsthaus Zurich, Fondation Beyeler in Basel, and Kunstmuseum Bern are renowned institutions.

3. Cultural Heritage:

UNESCO World Heritage Sites: Switzerland is home to several UNESCO World Heritage Sites that preserve its cultural and natural heritage. These include the Old

Town of Bern, the Lavaux vineyards on Lake Geneva, the Abbey of St. Gallen, and the Jungfrau-Aletsch-Bietschhorn region.

Music and Performing Arts: Switzerland has a rich musical heritage, with classical composers like Frank Martin and Othmar Schoeck hailing from the country. The Montreux Jazz Festival is an internationally acclaimed event, attracting top musicians from around the world. The Zurich Opera House and Lucerne Festival are renowned for their performances.

Traditional Festivals: Switzerland celebrates numerous traditional festivals throughout the year, each with its unique customs, costumes, music, and dance. The Fête de l'Escalade in Geneva, the Basel Carnival, and the Sechseläuten in Zurich are among the most famous.

Switzerland's cultural heritage, art, and architecture are a testament to its diverse influences, from Roman, Gothic, and Renaissance periods to modern and contemporary styles. Whether exploring historical landmarks, visiting art museums, or experiencing traditional festivities, Switzerland offers a captivating journey through its cultural legacy.

Chapter 2.
The Switzerland's top attractions

Eiger/Jungfraujoch

It is often referred to as the "Top of Europe" because it is the highest railway station in Europe, situated at an elevation of 3,454 meters (11,332 feet) above sea level. The location offers breathtaking panoramic views of the surrounding mountains, including the famous Eiger, Mönch, and Jungfrau peaks.

To reach Eiger/Jungfraujoch, visitors typically start their journey from Interlaken, a nearby town in the Swiss Alps. From Interlaken, they take a series of trains to reach the final destination. The journey involves changing trains at Kleine Scheidegg and then boarding the Jungfrau Railway, which takes passengers through a tunnel carved into the mountains to the Jungfraujoch station.

The opening and closing times of Eiger/Jungfraujoch can vary depending on the season and weather conditions. Generally, the attraction is open year-round, but certain facilities may have restricted access during specific periods. It is always recommended to check the official website or contact the tourist information centers for the most up-to-date information.

During the peak tourist season, which is typically from late spring to early autumn (June to September), Eiger/Jungfraujoch is usually fully operational. The trains to the top run frequently, allowing visitors to experience the stunning views and explore the various attractions at the station.

In terms of specific hours of operation, the first train from Kleine Scheidegg to Jungfraujoch typically departs early in the morning, around 6:00 or 6:30 a.m. The journey takes approximately one hour. The last train from Jungfraujoch back to Kleine Scheidegg leaves in the late afternoon, around 4:30 or 5:00 p.m. However, these times can vary, and it is advisable to check the current train schedule beforehand.

It's important to note that weather conditions play a significant role in the operation of Eiger/Jungfraujoch. The area is known for its unpredictable and rapidly changing weather, including fog, snow, and high winds. In case of inclement weather, train services may be temporarily suspended or delayed for safety reasons. It is advisable to monitor weather forecasts and make necessary adjustments to travel plans accordingly.

Lenzberg Castle

Lenzburg Castle, also known as Schloss Lenzburg, is a medieval castle located in the town of Lenzburg in the Aargau canton of Switzerland. It is one of the most important castles in the country and holds great historical and cultural significance. Lenzburg Castle sits atop a hill overlooking the town and offers stunning views of the surrounding landscape.

The castle has a rich history dating back over a thousand years. It was first mentioned in historical records in the 11th century and has since undergone various modifications and additions over the centuries. Originally built as a fortress, Lenzburg Castle served as a residence for the influential Lenzburg family, who were local nobles in the region.

Over time, ownership of the castle changed hands multiple times, and each owner made their own architectural contributions to the structure. Notable modifications include the addition of towers, residential wings, and defensive walls. The castle represents a mix of architectural styles, including Romanesque, Gothic, and Renaissance elements.

Today, Lenzburg Castle is open to the public and serves as a museum and cultural center. Visitors can explore the castle's interior, which showcases various exhibitions related to the castle's history, the region's heritage, and medieval life. The museum displays artifacts, artworks, and interactive exhibits that provide insights into the castle's past.

The castle grounds also feature beautiful gardens, courtyards, and a well-preserved castle chapel. These outdoor spaces are often used for cultural events, concerts, and special exhibitions. Additionally, the castle offers guided tours that provide in-depth information about its architecture, historical significance, and the daily lives of its former inhabitants.

Lenzburg Castle is typically open throughout the year, with specific opening hours varying by season. During the summer months (April to October), it is generally open from 10:00 a.m. to 5:00 p.m., and during the winter months (November to March), it may have reduced hours or be closed on certain days. It is advisable to check the official website or contact the castle directly to obtain the most up-to-date information regarding opening hours and admission fees.

Zurigo, Zugo

Zurich (Zurigo):

Zurich is the largest city in Switzerland and serves as the country's financial and economic hub. Located in the north-central part of Switzerland, Zurich is situated on the shores of Lake Zurich and is surrounded by picturesque mountains. The city is known for its cleanliness, efficiency, and high standard of living.

Zurich offers a mix of modernity and rich history. The city center, known as the Altstadt (Old Town), features narrow cobblestone streets, medieval buildings, and charming squares. Here, you can explore historical landmarks such as Fraumünster Church, Grossmünster Church, and the Lindenhof hill.

Aside from its historical sites, Zurich is also renowned for its thriving cultural scene. The city boasts numerous museums, art galleries, theaters, and music venues. It hosts various festivals throughout the year, including the Street Parade, Zurich Film Festival, and Zürcher Theater Spektakel. Shopping enthusiasts can explore the famous Bahnhofstrasse, a vibrant street known for its luxury boutiques and department stores.

Zurich is well-connected with an efficient public transportation system, including trams, buses, and trains. It is also a major transportation hub, with Zurich Airport (Flughafen Zürich) serving as one of the busiest airports in Europe.

Zug (Zugo):

Zug is a small, picturesque city located in central Switzerland. It is situated on the northeastern shore of Lake Zug and is surrounded by rolling hills and forests. Zug is known for its scenic beauty, low taxes, and being a major financial center.

Despite its smaller size, Zug has gained international recognition as a hub for various multinational companies, particularly in the fields of finance, commodities trading, and technology. The city's low corporate taxes have attracted many businesses to establish their headquarters or offices in Zug.

Zug's charming old town, known as Altstadt, is characterized by its well-preserved medieval buildings, narrow streets, and beautiful waterfront promenade. The city also offers a range of cultural attractions, including museums, art galleries, and theaters. In addition, Zug hosts several events and festivals throughout the year, such as the Zug Castle Festival and the Zuger Seefest (Lake Zug Festival).

With its convenient location, Zug provides easy access to other parts of Switzerland. It has a well-developed public transportation system, including trains and buses, making it an ideal base for exploring the surrounding regions.

San Gallo

San Gallo, also known as St. Gallen, is a city located in northeastern Switzerland. It is the capital of the canton of St. Gallen and holds both historical and cultural significance. The city is named after Saint Gall, an Irish monk who established a hermitage in the region in the 7th century.

San Gallo is renowned for its well-preserved medieval architecture and its picturesque setting at the foot of the Appenzell Alps. The city's Altstadt (Old Town) is a UNESCO World Heritage Site and is considered one of the most beautiful in Switzerland. Its narrow cobblestone streets, colorful buildings, and ornate facades create a charming atmosphere. The Abbey of St. Gall, a majestic Benedictine monastery founded in the 8th century, is a major highlight of the city. The abbey library, with its vast collection of ancient manuscripts, is particularly notable.

Aside from its historical and architectural treasures, San Gallo offers a range of cultural attractions. The city is home to several museums, including the Kunstmuseum St. Gallen (Art Museum), which houses a diverse collection of contemporary and modern art. The Textile Museum showcases the city's rich textile industry history, and the Natural History Museum features exhibits on the region's flora, fauna, and geology.

San Gallo is also known for its vibrant cultural scene. The city hosts various events and festivals throughout the year, including the St. Gallen Festival, which is a renowned music and theater festival. The Olma Fair, held annually, showcases agriculture, livestock, and regional products and traditions.

The University of St. Gallen, a prestigious institution specializing in business, economics, law, and social sciences, adds to the city's academic and intellectual atmosphere. The university's campus features modern architecture and beautiful surroundings.

San Gallo offers excellent transportation connections. It has a well-developed public transportation system, including trains and buses, making it easy to explore both the city and the surrounding region. Additionally, the city is located close to the Lake Constance (Bodensee) region, which is known for its natural beauty and recreational opportunities.

Basilea

Basilea, or Basel in English, is a city located in northwest Switzerland. It is the third-largest city in the country and holds great cultural, historical, and economic significance. Basel is situated on the banks of the Rhine River, near the borders of Germany and France, making it a vibrant and multicultural city.

Basel is known for its rich history and architectural beauty. The city's Altstadt (Old Town) features well-preserved medieval buildings, narrow cobblestone streets, and charming squares. The impressive Basel Minster, a Gothic cathedral dating back to the 12th century, dominates the city's skyline. The old city walls, gateways, and historic landmarks such as the Rathaus (Town Hall) contribute to Basel's historical charm.

The city is a hub of art and culture, boasting numerous museums and galleries. The Kunstmuseum Basel, one of the oldest public art collections in the world, houses an extensive collection of European art from the Middle Ages to contemporary works. The Fondation Beyeler, located just outside the city, showcases modern and contemporary art in a stunning building surrounded by beautiful gardens.

Basel is renowned for its vibrant cultural scene and hosts various events and festivals throughout the year. The most famous of these is Art Basel, one of the world's premier contemporary art fairs, attracting art enthusiasts and collectors from around the globe. Basel also celebrates Fasnacht, a lively carnival held in February, known for its elaborate costumes, parades, and traditional music.

The city is a major center for pharmaceutical and chemical industries, and it hosts the headquarters of several multinational companies. Basel is also home to the University of Basel, one of Switzerland's oldest universities, known for its research and academic excellence.

The Rhine River adds to Basel's appeal, providing opportunities for scenic boat trips, leisurely walks along the riverbanks, and water-based activities. Basel's location near the borders of Germany and France makes it an ideal base for exploring the nearby regions, including the Black Forest and the Alsace wine region.

Basel has excellent transportation connections, including an international airport and a well-developed public transportation system. The city's efficient trams and buses make it easy to navigate and explore its various attractions.

Grindelwald

Grindelwald is a picturesque alpine village located in the Bernese Alps of Switzerland. Nestled in the Jungfrau region, it is renowned for its stunning mountain scenery, outdoor activities, and access to the Jungfrau mountain range.

Grindelwald is surrounded by towering peaks, including the famous Eiger, Mönch, and Jungfrau mountains. The village itself has a charming, traditional Swiss ambiance with wooden chalets, flower-filled balconies, and a tranquil atmosphere. Its location provides breathtaking views of the surrounding mountains, glaciers, and lush valleys.

One of the main attractions in Grindelwald is the Jungfrau Railway, which is accessed from Kleine Scheidegg, a mountain pass near the village. This railway takes visitors on a scenic journey through tunnels carved into the mountains, offering spectacular vistas of snow-capped peaks, glaciers, and deep valleys. At the top, visitors reach the Jungfraujoch, also known as the "Top of Europe," which is the highest railway station in Europe. Here, you can enjoy panoramic views, visit the Ice Palace, and explore the various attractions and restaurants.

Grindelwald is a paradise for outdoor enthusiasts. In the summer, the region offers a wide range of activities, including hiking, mountain biking, paragliding, and climbing. There are numerous trails that cater to different levels of difficulty, leading to viewpoints, mountain lakes, and scenic landscapes. The First Cliff Walk, a suspension bridge on the First Mountain, provides an exhilarating experience and panoramic views of the surrounding peaks.

During the winter months, Grindelwald transforms into a popular ski resort. The region offers excellent skiing and snowboarding opportunities with a variety of slopes for all skill levels. The interconnected ski areas of Grindelwald-First, Kleine Scheidegg-Männlichen, and Mürren-Schilthorn provide a vast network of trails and breathtaking descents. There are also options for cross-country skiing, snowshoeing, and ice climbing.

In addition to outdoor activities, Grindelwald has a range of amenities, including hotels, restaurants, cafes, and shops. The village maintains its traditional Alpine charm and offers a warm and welcoming atmosphere for visitors.

Grindelwald is easily accessible by train from major Swiss cities such as Zurich, Bern, and Geneva. There are regular train connections to the village, and a well-developed transportation system within the region allows for easy exploration of nearby areas and attractions.

Friburgo

Friburgo, also known as Fribourg (French) or Freiburg (German), is a charming city located in the western part of Switzerland. It serves as the capital of the canton of Fribourg and sits on a plateau above the Sarine River. Friburgo is known for its well-preserved medieval old town, bilingualism, and rich cultural heritage.

The city of Friburgo showcases a unique blend of French and German influences due to its location on the linguistic border between the French-speaking and German-speaking regions of Switzerland. As a result, both French and German are widely spoken, and street signs and official documents are presented in both languages.

The old town of Friburgo is a major attraction, featuring narrow cobblestone streets, medieval buildings with intricate facades, and a picturesque setting along the Sarine River. The Cathedral of Saint Nicholas, a magnificent Gothic cathedral dating back to the 13th century, dominates the city's skyline. Visitors can climb the tower for panoramic views of the city and surrounding countryside.

Wandering through the old town, you'll encounter charming squares, fountains, and arcades that house shops, cafes, and restaurants. The Zaehringen Bridge, a wooden bridge dating back to the 13th century, connects the old town with the newer parts of the city and offers stunning views of the river and the cityscape.

Friburgo is also known for its rich cultural scene. The University of Fribourg, founded in 1889, is one of the leading academic institutions in Switzerland and contributes to the city's vibrant intellectual atmosphere. The city hosts various cultural events, including music festivals, art exhibitions, and theater performances. The Espace Jean Tinguely - Niki de Saint Phalle, located in the neighboring city of Fribourg, is a museum dedicated to the works of renowned Swiss artist Jean Tinguely and French-American sculptor Niki de Saint Phalle.

In terms of gastronomy, Friburgo offers a variety of culinary delights. Local specialties include Swiss cheeses, such as Gruyère and Vacherin, and the traditional Swiss fondue is a must-try. The city is also known for its chocolate and sweets, with numerous confectioneries and chocolate shops scattered throughout.

Friburgo benefits from its central location, making it a convenient base for exploring the surrounding areas. The pre-Alpine region of Schwarzsee, the Gruyère region with its famous cheese and castle, and the beautiful Bernese Oberland are all within easy reach.

Friburgo can be reached by train from major Swiss cities, and the city itself has a well-developed public transportation system, including buses and a funicular, which makes it easy to get around.

Ginevra

Ginevra, or Geneva in English, is a cosmopolitan city located in the westernmost part of Switzerland. It is situated on the banks of Lake Geneva (Lac Léman) and is surrounded by the picturesque Swiss Alps. Geneva is known as a global hub for diplomacy, finance, and international organizations.

The city is home to several international organizations and is often referred to as the "Capital of Peace." The headquarters of the United Nations in Europe, as well as numerous other international agencies such as the World Health Organization (WHO) and the International Red Cross and Red Crescent Museum, are located in Geneva. The city hosts important diplomatic negotiations and is known for its role in promoting humanitarian efforts and international cooperation.

Geneva is also known for its natural beauty and its stunning location on the shores of Lake Geneva. The lake provides a picturesque backdrop to the city, and its clear waters offer opportunities for various water-based activities, including boat cruises, swimming, and paddleboarding. The famous Jet d'Eau, a water fountain located on the lake, is one of the city's most iconic landmarks.

The old town of Geneva, known as the Vieille Ville, is a charming area with narrow streets, historic buildings, and quaint squares. St. Peter's Cathedral, a prominent Gothic-style cathedral dating back to the 12th century, is a major attraction in the old town. The Place du Bourg-de-Four, one of the oldest squares in Geneva, is a bustling gathering place with outdoor cafes and restaurants.

Geneva is renowned for its high quality of life and its commitment to culture and the arts. The city offers a wide range of museums, art galleries, and theaters. The Museum of Art and History showcases a diverse collection of art and artifacts, including works by renowned artists such as Rembrandt and Monet. The Grand Théâtre de Genève hosts opera, ballet, and theater performances.

The city is known for its culinary scene, offering a wide variety of international cuisines as well as Swiss specialties. Chocolate lovers can indulge in exquisite Swiss chocolates, and cheese enthusiasts can savor local favorites such as Gruyère and Emmental.

Geneva is well-connected with an extensive public transportation system, including buses, trams, and trains. It is also served by an international airport, making it easily accessible for visitors from around the world.

The Matterhorn

The Matterhorn is one of the most iconic and recognizable mountains in the world. It is located in the Pennine Alps on the border between Switzerland and Italy. With its distinctive pyramid shape and towering presence, the Matterhorn is a symbol of the Swiss Alps and attracts mountaineers, outdoor enthusiasts, and tourists from around the globe.

Here are some key facts and features about the Matterhorn:

Geography: The Matterhorn stands at an elevation of 4,478 meters (14,692 feet) above sea level. It is part of the Pennine Alps and is situated in the Swiss canton of Valais and the Italian region of Aosta Valley. The mountain is surrounded by other famous peaks, including the Dent d'Hérens and the Monte Rosa massif.

Distinctive Shape: The Matterhorn's unique shape is characterized by four steep faces that face the compass points (north, south, east, and west). It has a sharp, pyramidal summit with a distinct horn-like appearance, which is how it acquired its name—Matterhorn translates to "meadow peak" in German.

Mountaineering History: The Matterhorn is renowned for its challenging and treacherous climbing routes. Its first ascent was successfully completed on July 14, 1865, by a seven-member team led by British climber Edward Whymper. However, tragedy struck during the descent, resulting in the death of four climbers. This event marked a turning point in the history of mountaineering and led to improved safety measures and climbing techniques.

Tourism and Scenic Beauty: The Matterhorn's grandeur and picturesque setting make it a major tourist attraction. The town of Zermatt, situated at the foot of the mountain on the Swiss side, serves as a popular base for visitors. From Zermatt, cable cars and cogwheel trains transport tourists to vantage points, such as Gornergrat and Rothorn, offering breathtaking views of the Matterhorn and the surrounding alpine scenery.

Winter Sports: Zermatt and the nearby region offer excellent opportunities for winter sports enthusiasts. The area boasts a vast network of ski slopes, with Zermatt being renowned for its extensive ski area and reliable snow conditions. Skiing, snowboarding, and other winter activities can be enjoyed against the backdrop of the majestic Matterhorn.

Symbolic Significance: The Matterhorn has become a symbol of Swiss excellence, beauty, and precision. Its distinct shape has been used in various logos, advertisements, and Swiss chocolate packaging, further enhancing its recognition and iconic status.

Preservation and Conservation: The preservation of the Matterhorn and its surrounding natural environment is a priority. The mountain is part of a protected area and efforts are made to ensure sustainable tourism practices and maintain its pristine beauty for future generations.

Whether admired from afar or experienced up close, the Matterhorn captivates with its awe-inspiring presence, mountaineering history, and stunning alpine scenery. It remains a must-see destination for nature lovers, outdoor enthusiasts, and those seeking the thrill of alpine adventure.

Lake Geneva

Lake Geneva, known as Lac Léman in French, is a large and stunning lake located on the border between Switzerland and France. It is the largest lake in Western Europe and stretches approximately 70 kilometers (45 miles) in length. Lake Geneva is surrounded by picturesque landscapes, charming towns, and snow-capped mountains, making it a popular tourist destination.

Here are some key features and attractions of Lake Geneva:

Geography: Lake Geneva is nestled in a basin formed by the Rhône River, with the Alps to the east and the Jura Mountains to the northwest. The lake is shared by both Switzerland and France, with the French departments of Haute-Savoie and Ain bordering its southern shores. The lake's depth reaches up to 310 meters (1,017 feet), making it one of the deepest lakes in Europe.

Scenic Beauty: Lake Geneva is renowned for its breathtaking beauty. The crystal-clear blue waters of the lake are framed by majestic mountains, including the famous Mont Blanc, the highest peak in the Alps. The lake's shoreline is adorned with lush vineyards, charming villages, and luxurious waterfront estates.

Lausanne: Lausanne, the capital of the Swiss canton of Vaud, is located on the northern shores of Lake Geneva. This vibrant city offers a rich cultural heritage, with historical landmarks, museums, and a lively atmosphere. Lausanne is home to the International Olympic Committee headquarters and hosts various sports and cultural events.

Geneva: Geneva, situated at the southwestern tip of the lake, is another prominent city that shares its name with the lake itself. Known as the "Capital of Peace," Geneva hosts numerous international organizations, including the United Nations and the Red Cross. The city boasts a picturesque waterfront, a charming old town, and a reputation for luxury shopping and fine dining.

Montreux: Montreux, located on the northeastern shore of the lake, is famous for its annual Montreux Jazz Festival, which attracts renowned musicians from around the world. The town is known for its mild climate and stunning promenade, which offers panoramic views of the lake and the surrounding mountains.

Water Activities: Lake Geneva provides ample opportunities for various water-based activities. Sailing, boating, and windsurfing are popular, and there are rental services available for those who wish to explore the lake's beauty. Swimming is also possible in designated areas during the summer months.

Vineyards and Wine: The region around Lake Geneva is known for its vineyards and wine production. The terraced vineyards along the lake's shores produce excellent wines, particularly white wines. Wine enthusiasts can explore the wine-growing regions, visit wineries, and indulge in wine tastings.

The lake is easily accessible, with several towns and cities situated along its shores offering transportation connections, including train services, boat cruises, and road networks. These enable visitors to explore the various attractions and destinations around Lake Geneva.

Matterhorn Glacier Paradise

Matterhorn Glacier Paradise, also known as Klein Matterhorn, is a popular tourist attraction located in the Zermatt region of Switzerland. It is a high-altitude mountain peak and offers visitors breathtaking views, year-round snow, and a range of activities.

Here are some key details about Matterhorn Glacier Paradise:

Location: Matterhorn Glacier Paradise is situated on the southern side of the Swiss-Italian border in the Pennine Alps. It is accessed via a series of cable cars from Zermatt, a picturesque town at the base of the Matterhorn mountain.

Altitude and Views: At an elevation of 3,883 meters (12,740 feet), Matterhorn Glacier Paradise is one of the highest points accessible to tourists in the Swiss Alps. The summit offers panoramic views of the surrounding mountains, including the Matterhorn, Monte Rosa, and several other impressive peaks.

Year-Round Snow and Skiing: Thanks to its high altitude, Matterhorn Glacier Paradise has snow-covered slopes and skiing opportunities throughout the year. Visitors can enjoy skiing, snowboarding, and other snow activities even during the summer months. The ski area offers a variety of slopes suitable for different skill levels, and equipment rental is available.

Ice Palace: One of the highlights of Matterhorn Glacier Paradise is the Ice Palace, a fascinating underground world of ice and ice sculptures. Visitors can explore the corridors and chambers of the palace, admiring the intricate ice carvings and learning about glaciology.

Observation Deck: The summit of Matterhorn Glacier Paradise features an observation deck with 360-degree panoramic views. From here, visitors can take in the stunning alpine scenery, including the Matterhorn, the surrounding peaks, and the vast expanse of glaciers.

Restaurants and Facilities: Matterhorn Glacier Paradise offers various facilities for visitors' comfort and enjoyment. There are several restaurants and cafes where visitors can savor Swiss cuisine and take in the magnificent views. Additionally, there are souvenir shops, restrooms, and other amenities available.

Accessibility and Tickets: To reach Matterhorn Glacier Paradise, visitors need to take a series of cable cars from Zermatt. The journey involves multiple stages, including transfers at Trockener Steg and Schwarzsee. It is recommended to check the operating hours and ticket prices in advance, as they may vary depending on the season and weather conditions.

Matterhorn Glacier Paradise provides an extraordinary opportunity to experience the beauty of the Swiss Alps and enjoy a range of snow activities throughout the year. The combination of awe-inspiring views, the Ice Palace, and the chance to stand atop a high-altitude summit make it a memorable destination for nature and adventure enthusiasts.

Chillon Castle

Chillon Castle, also known as Château de Chillon, is a stunning medieval fortress located on the shores of Lake Geneva in Switzerland. It is situated near the town of Montreux in the canton of Vaud and is one of the most visited historic sites in the country.

Here are some key details about Chillon Castle:

History: Chillon Castle has a rich and fascinating history that dates back over a thousand years. It was built during the 11th century and served as a strategic fortress controlling the passage along Lake Geneva. Over the centuries, the castle underwent several modifications and expansions. It was also used as a residence for the Counts of Savoy and later as a prison.

Architecture and Setting: The castle's architectural style is predominantly Gothic, with elements of Romanesque and Renaissance influences. It is situated on a rocky islet, connected to the mainland by a small bridge. The castle's location on the lake shore provides a picturesque backdrop, surrounded by the beauty of Lake Geneva and the mountains.

Features and Exhibitions: Chillon Castle consists of several buildings, including courtyards, towers, dungeons, and residential areas. The castle's interior is well-preserved and offers visitors a glimpse into medieval life. It features furnished rooms, including the Great Hall, the Duke's Bedroom, and the Gothic Chapel. There are also exhibits displaying medieval weapons, armor, and historical artifacts.

The Castle's Literary Connections: Chillon Castle gained literary fame through Lord Byron's poem "The Prisoner of Chillon." The poem recounts the story of François Bonivard, a political prisoner held in the castle during the 16th century. The poem brought attention to the castle and contributed to its popularity as a tourist destination.

Visiting Chillon Castle: Chillon Castle is open to the public, allowing visitors to explore its halls, chambers, and courtyards. Guided tours are available in multiple languages, providing historical and architectural insights. The castle also hosts temporary exhibitions, cultural events, and concerts, adding to its vibrant atmosphere.

Surrounding Area: The castle's location on the shores of Lake Geneva offers breathtaking views and recreational opportunities. Visitors can enjoy leisurely walks along the lake, relax on the nearby beaches, or take boat trips to explore the scenic surroundings. The town of Montreux, famous for its annual jazz festival, is just a short distance away.

Chillon Castle's combination of historical significance, architectural beauty, and stunning lakeside location make it a captivating destination for history enthusiasts, culture lovers, and those seeking to immerse themselves in Switzerland's medieval past.

Lake Lucerne

Lake Lucerne, also known as Lake Luzern or Vierwaldstättersee in German, is a picturesque lake located in central Switzerland. It is one of the country's most famous and visited lakes, offering stunning scenery, crystal-clear waters, and a wealth of recreational activities.

Here are some key details about Lake Lucerne:

Geography: Lake Lucerne is situated in the heart of Switzerland, surrounded by towering mountains and lush landscapes. It has a complex shape, with several arms or "fjords" extending into the surrounding valleys. The lake spans an area of about 114 square kilometers (44 square miles) and has a maximum depth of 214 meters (702 feet).

Beauty and Scenic Highlights: Lake Lucerne is known for its breathtaking beauty. The deep blue waters of the lake are complemented by the stunning backdrop of the Swiss Alps, including iconic peaks such as Mount Pilatus, Rigi, and Stanserhorn. The lake's shoreline is dotted with charming towns, picturesque villages, and historic landmarks.

Boat Cruises: Exploring Lake Lucerne by boat is a popular activity for visitors. Regular boat services operate throughout the year, allowing passengers to enjoy leisurely cruises on the lake while taking in the majestic mountain scenery. Boat trips often stop at various towns and villages along the lake, providing an opportunity to explore their attractions.

Rigi and Pilatus Mountains: Lake Lucerne is flanked by two famous mountains that offer panoramic views of the surrounding area. Mount Rigi, known as the "Queen of the Mountains," can be reached by a cogwheel railway from Vitznau or Arth-Goldau. Mount Pilatus, accessible from Lucerne, offers a cable car and cogwheel railway experience. Both mountains provide breathtaking vistas and hiking opportunities.

Water Sports and Recreation: Lake Lucerne offers a range of water-based activities for outdoor enthusiasts. Swimming, kayaking, paddleboarding, and sailing are popular pursuits during the summer months. The lake's clean and clear waters provide an ideal setting for water sports and leisurely lake-side strolls.

Lakeside Towns and Landmarks: Lake Lucerne is surrounded by several charming towns and landmarks worth exploring. Lucerne, the largest city on the lake, is renowned for its well-preserved medieval architecture, picturesque Old Town, and iconic Chapel Bridge.

Weggis, Vitznau, and Brunnen are among the other towns along the lake that offer scenic views, historic sites, and a variety of recreational opportunities.

Accessibility: Lake Lucerne is easily accessible from major Swiss cities such as Zurich and Basel. The towns around the lake are well-served by public transportation, including trains, buses, and boat services. Visitors can easily navigate the region and explore its various attractions.

Montreux Congress Palace

The Montreux Congress Palace, also known as the Montreux Convention Centre, is a renowned conference and event venue located in Montreux, Switzerland. Situated on the shores of Lake Geneva, it offers a beautiful setting and modern facilities for hosting a wide range of conferences, meetings, exhibitions, and cultural events.

Here are some key details about the Montreux Congress Palace:

Location and Setting: The Montreux Congress Palace is located in the heart of Montreux, a picturesque town on the eastern shore of Lake Geneva. The venue enjoys stunning panoramic views of the lake and the surrounding Alps, providing a scenic backdrop for events.

Facilities: The Montreux Congress Palace offers versatile facilities that can accommodate events of various sizes and types. The venue includes spacious conference halls, meeting rooms, exhibition areas, and banquet halls. The main auditorium, known as the Stravinski Auditorium, is a state-of-the-art concert hall with excellent acoustics, making it suitable for music performances and large conferences.Capacity and Flexibility: The Montreux Congress Palace can cater to both small and large events. The Stravinski Auditorium has a seating capacity of up to 2,000 people, while the venue's other rooms can accommodate smaller gatherings. The venue is equipped with modern audiovisual technology, internet connectivity, and other amenities to support different event requirements.

Event Hosting: The Montreux Congress Palace is a preferred venue for a wide range of events, including corporate conferences, seminars, trade shows, product launches, cultural festivals, and music concerts. It has a long history of hosting prestigious events, including the Montreux Jazz Festival, which takes place annually and attracts renowned musicians and music enthusiasts from around the world.

Location Advantages: Montreux is known for its accessibility and tourism infrastructure. The town is well-connected by train, road, and boat services, making it easily reachable from major Swiss cities and international airports. Montreux also offers a variety of accommodations, restaurants, and leisure activities, making it an attractive destination for event attendees.

Professional Support: The Montreux Congress Palace provides professional event management services and technical support to ensure the success of conferences and events. Their experienced team can assist with planning, logistics, audiovisual setup, catering, and other event-related services.

Rhine Falls

Rhine Falls, located in Switzerland, is one of the most famous waterfalls in Europe and a popular tourist destination. Here are some details about the Rhine Falls and its accessibility as a tourist site:

Location: Rhine Falls is situated on the High Rhine near the town of Schaffhausen in northern Switzerland. It is only a few kilometers away from the German border.

Size and Features: Rhine Falls is the largest waterfall in Europe by volume and offers a breathtaking sight as the mighty Rhine River plunges over a 23-meter (75-foot) high and 150-meter (490-foot) wide cliff. The falls are characterized by their impressive power and the roar of cascading water.

Accessibility: Rhine Falls is easily accessible from various parts of Switzerland and neighboring countries:

By Air: The nearest major airport is Zurich Airport (ZRH), which is approximately 45 kilometers (28 miles) away from Rhine Falls. From there, you can take a train or rent a car to reach the falls.

By Train: Schaffhausen, the closest town to Rhine Falls, is well-connected by train. Regular train services operate from Zurich, Basel, and other major Swiss cities to Schaffhausen. From the Schaffhausen train station, you can take a bus, taxi, or walk to the falls (around 2 kilometers or 1.2 miles).

By Car: If you prefer to drive, Rhine Falls is easily accessible by car. There are parking facilities available near the falls, and it takes approximately 30 minutes to drive from Zurich to Rhine Falls.

Visitor Facilities: Rhine Falls offers several amenities to enhance the tourist experience:

Observation Decks: There are several observation decks strategically positioned to provide different vantage points of the falls. Visitors can get close to the cascades and feel the spray of the water.

Boat Trips: Boat tours are available, allowing visitors to experience the falls up close. These trips take you to a rock in the middle of the falls called the "Rheinfallfelsen" and offer a unique perspective of the roaring water.

Visitor Center: The Rhine Falls Visitor Center provides information about the falls, its geological formation, and the surrounding area. It also houses a restaurant, souvenir shops, and restrooms.

Accessibility: Rhine Falls aims to be accessible to people with disabilities. There are wheelchair-friendly paths and lifts available to ensure that everyone can enjoy the natural wonder.

Nearby Attractions: In addition to visiting Rhine Falls, you can explore other attractions in the region. Schaffhausen, the nearby town, boasts a well-preserved medieval old town with charming streets, historical buildings, and museums. The Munot fortress, overlooking the town, offers panoramic views of the area.

Overall, Rhine Falls in Switzerland is an awe-inspiring natural wonder easily accessible to tourists. Whether you're interested in the sheer power of the falls, boat trips, or exploring the surrounding region, Rhine Falls offers a memorable experience for visitors of all ages.

Bellinzona Castle

Belinzona, located in the Italian-speaking canton of Ticino, Switzerland, is home to a collection of three stunning castles known as the Castles of Bellinzona. Here are some details about the Bellinzona Castles and their accessibility as a tourist site:

Location: The Bellinzona Castles are situated in the town of Bellinzona, which is located in the southern part of Switzerland, near the border with Italy. The town is easily accessible from major Swiss cities such as Zurich, Geneva, and Bern.

History and UNESCO World Heritage Site: The Bellinzona Castles have a rich history dating back to the Middle Ages. The three castles—Castelgrande, Montebello, and Sasso Corbaro—were strategically positioned to guard the Alpine passes. Due to their historical and architectural significance, the Castles of

Bellinzona were designated as a UNESCO World Heritage Site in 2000.

Accessibility: The Bellinzona Castles are easily accessible for tourists:

By Train: Bellinzona is well-connected by train, and there are regular services from major Swiss cities. The castles are within walking distance (around 10-15 minutes) from the Bellinzona train station.

By Car: If you prefer to drive, Bellinzona is easily accessible by car. The town is located at the intersection of major highways and has parking facilities near the castles.

By Foot: The castles are within close proximity to each other, making it convenient to explore them on foot. There are pedestrian paths and signs guiding visitors to the different castles.

Castles of Bellinzona:

Castelgrande: This is the oldest and largest of the three castles. It is located on a rocky hill and offers panoramic views of the town and the surrounding area. Castelgrande houses a museum that showcases the history and architecture of the castles.

Montebello: Situated on a nearby hill, Montebello Castle is characterized by its cylindrical shape and imposing presence. It provides insights into medieval military architecture and offers scenic views of the town and the Alps.

Sasso Corbaro: Positioned on a rocky ridge, Sasso Corbaro Castle is the highest of the three castles. It is known for its well-preserved fortifications and houses a museum that exhibits arms and armor from the Middle Ages.

Visitor Facilities: The Bellinzona Castles provide several amenities for visitors:

Guided Tours: Guided tours are available in multiple languages, allowing visitors to learn about the history, architecture, and cultural significance of the castles.

Visitor Centers: Each castle has its own visitor center with informative displays, exhibitions, and facilities such as restrooms.

Accessibility: Efforts have been made to improve accessibility at the castles. However, due to their historical nature and hilltop locations, some areas may have limited accessibility for people with mobility issues.

Events and Festivals: Throughout the year, the Castles of Bellinzona host various cultural events, including medieval festivals, concerts, and exhibitions, which offer a unique experience for visitors.

The Bellinzona Castles in Switzerland are not only historically significant but also offer stunning views and insights into medieval architecture. With their accessibility and range of visitor facilities, the castles provide an enriching experience for tourists interested in history, culture, and picturesque landscapes.

International Museum of the Red Cross and Red Crescent

The International Museum of the Red Cross and Red Crescent is a renowned museum located in Geneva, Switzerland. Here are some details about the museum and its accessibility as a tourist site:

Location: The museum is situated in Geneva, Switzerland, on the grounds of the headquarters of the International Committee of the Red Cross (ICRC) and the International Federation of Red Cross and Red Crescent Societies (IFRC).

Purpose and Focus: The International Museum of the Red Cross and Red Crescent aims to promote humanitarian principles, raise awareness about the activities of the Red Cross and Red Crescent Movement, and educate visitors about the consequences of armed conflicts and natural disasters.

Exhibitions and Collections: The museum offers a range of exhibits and collections that explore the history, work, and impact of the Red Cross and Red Crescent Movement. Some notable features include:

Permanent Exhibition: The permanent exhibition presents a comprehensive overview of the humanitarian work carried out by the Red Cross and Red Crescent. It covers topics such as humanitarian aid, international humanitarian law, health, and the challenges faced by people affected by armed conflicts and disasters.

Temporary Exhibitions: The museum hosts temporary exhibitions that delve into specific aspects of humanitarian work, historical events, and the contributions of individuals and organizations.

Archives and Documentation Center: The museum houses an extensive collection of archives, photographs, and audiovisual materials related to the Red Cross and Red Crescent Movement, making it a valuable resource for researchers and scholars.

Accessibility: The International Museum of the Red Cross and Red Crescent is easily accessible for tourists:

By Public Transport: Geneva has an excellent public transportation system, including buses and trams. The museum is well-connected and can be reached easily using public transport.

By Car: If you prefer to drive, there are parking facilities available near the museum. However, it's worth noting that parking in Geneva can be limited and expensive.

Accessibility within the Museum: The museum is designed to be accessible to people with disabilities. It offers facilities such as elevators, ramps, accessible restrooms, and wheelchair-friendly paths to ensure that all visitors can enjoy the exhibits.

Visitor Facilities: The museum provides several amenities to enhance the visitor experience:

Guided Tours: Guided tours are available in multiple languages, providing in-depth insights into the exhibits and the work of the Red Cross and Red Crescent Movement.

Audio Guides: Audio guides are available for rent, offering additional information and commentary on the exhibitions.

Museum Shop: The museum has a shop where visitors can purchase books, souvenirs, and items related to humanitarian work.

Café: There is a café on-site where visitors can relax and enjoy refreshments.

Events and Activities: The museum organizes various events, conferences, and educational programs related to humanitarian work and international humanitarian law..

Old Town Bern

The Old Town of Bern, also known as the UNESCO World Heritage Site of "Bern's Old City," is a captivating and well-preserved medieval town located in the capital city of Switzerland. Here are some details about the Old Town of Bern and its accessibility as a tourist site:

Location: The Old Town of Bern is situated in the heart of the city of Bern, Switzerland. It is located on a peninsula surrounded by the Aare River and is easily accessible from various parts of the city.

History and Architecture: The Old Town of Bern dates back to the 12th century and is renowned for its well-preserved medieval architecture. It showcases a harmonious blend of Gothic and Renaissance styles, characterized by sandstone buildings, narrow streets, arcades, and fountains. The town's layout and architecture have remained largely unchanged over the centuries.

Accessibility: The Old Town of Bern is easily accessible for tourists:

By Public Transport: Bern has an excellent public transportation system, including trams and buses. The Old Town is well-served by public transport, with several tram and bus stops located nearby.

By Train: Bern is a major transportation hub in Switzerland, and the main train station, Bern Hauptbahnhof, is located just outside the Old Town. From the train station, it is a short walk to the Old Town.

By Car: If you prefer to drive, there are parking facilities available near the Old Town. However, it's worth noting that driving in the Old Town can be challenging due to narrow streets and traffic restrictions. It is recommended to park outside the Old Town and walk in.

Accessibility within the Old Town: While the Old Town's medieval layout presents some challenges for accessibility, efforts have been made to improve accessibility for visitors with mobility issues. There are wheelchair-friendly paths, ramps, and elevators in certain areas, and some buildings have accessible entrances. However, due to the historic nature of the town, not all buildings and attractions may be fully accessible.

Main Attractions: The Old Town of Bern offers a wealth of attractions and points of interest for tourists:

Zytglogge (Clock Tower): This iconic clock tower dates back to the 13th century and features an astronomical clock that puts on a captivating show every hour.

Bundeshaus (Federal Palace): The Federal Palace is the seat of the Swiss Federal Assembly and the Federal Council. Visitors can take guided tours to explore the building and learn about Swiss politics.

Bern Cathedral (Münster): This impressive Gothic cathedral dominates the skyline of Bern. Visitors can climb the tower for panoramic views of the city.

Bear Park (BärenPark): Located just outside the Old Town, the Bear Park is home to Bern's beloved symbol, the bears. It provides a natural habitat for the bears to roam and is a popular attraction for visitors.

Historical Museums: The Old Town houses several museums, including the Bern Historical Museum, Einstein House, and Museum of Communication, where visitors can delve into the city's history, culture, and notable figures.

Pedestrian Zone: The Old Town of Bern is largely a pedestrian zone, making it easy to explore on foot. The compact size of the town allows visitors to wander through the charming streets, admire the architecture, and discover hidden corners and historical landmarks.

Shops and Restaurants: The Old Town is also known for its vibrant shopping scene. The arcades (Lauben) are lined with boutiques, shops, and cafés, offering a mix of international brands and local specialties. Visitors can savor Swiss cuisine at traditional restaurants or enjoy a coffee in one of the cozy cafés.

Mount Pilatus

Mount Pilatus is a majestic mountain located in the Swiss Alps, near the city of Lucerne in Switzerland. Here are some details about Mount Pilatus and its accessibility as a tourist site:

Location: Mount Pilatus is situated in central Switzerland, overlooking the beautiful Lake Lucerne. It is easily accessible from Lucerne, which is a popular tourist destination in its own right.

Scenic Beauty: Mount Pilatus is known for its breathtaking natural beauty, offering panoramic views of the surrounding Alps, lakes, and forests. It features rugged peaks, deep valleys, and picturesque landscapes, making it a favorite spot for nature enthusiasts and photographers.

Accessibility: Mount Pilatus is accessible for tourists:

By Public Transport: The most convenient way to reach Mount Pilatus is by using public transportation. From Lucerne, you can take a boat across Lake Lucerne to Alpnachstad, where you can board the world's steepest cogwheel railway, known as the Pilatus Railway, which takes you to the summit. Alternatively, you can take a bus from Lucerne to Kriens, where you can hop on the Pilatus Cable Car to reach the top.

By Car: If you prefer to drive, you can reach Mount Pilatus by car. There are parking facilities available at both Alpnachstad and Kriens, where you can start your ascent.

Accessibility within the Mountain: Mount Pilatus provides various facilities to ensure accessibility for all visitors. The Pilatus Railway and the Pilatus Cable Car are designed to accommodate people with disabilities. At the summit, there are wheelchair-accessible paths and facilities, including restaurants, restrooms, and viewing platforms.

Activities and Attractions: Mount Pilatus offers a range of activities and attractions for tourists:

Hiking: There are numerous hiking trails on Mount Pilatus, catering to different fitness levels. These trails allow you to explore the mountain's natural beauty and enjoy the fresh Alpine air.

Panoramic Views: From the summit, you can enjoy breathtaking panoramic views of the Swiss Alps, Lake Lucerne, and the surrounding landscapes. On clear days, you can even see as far as the Black Forest in Germany and the Mont Blanc massif in France.

Cable Car and Cogwheel Railway: The Pilatus Cable Car and Pilatus Railway provide a memorable journey to the summit, offering stunning views along the way. These rides are attractions in themselves, showcasing the engineering marvels of Swiss mountain transport.

Dragon Ride: The Dragon Ride is a unique aerial cableway that takes you from Fräkmüntegg to Pilatus Kulm. It offers a thrilling experience and magnificent views during the ascent.

Restaurants and Souvenir Shops: At the summit, there are several restaurants where you can savor Swiss cuisine while enjoying the views. There are also souvenir shops where you can purchase mementos of your visit.

Weather and Seasonal Considerations: It's important to check the weather conditions before visiting Mount Pilatus, as it can affect accessibility and visibility. The mountain is open to visitors from late spring to autumn, and some activities, such as hiking, may be limited or closed during the winter months.

Gruyeres Castle

picturesque town of Gruyères in the canton of Fribourg, Switzerland. Here are some details about Gruyères Castle and its accessibility as a tourist site:

Location: Gruyères Castle is situated in the town of Gruyères, which is nestled in the Swiss Pre-Alps. The town is easily accessible by train or car from major Swiss cities such as Geneva, Zurich, and Bern.

History and Architecture: Gruyères Castle dates back to the 13th century and is a fine example of medieval architecture. It features a well-preserved exterior with fortified walls, towers, and a central courtyard. The castle has undergone several renovations over the years and now houses a museum.

Accessibility: Gruyères Castle is accessible for tourists:

By Public Transport: Gruyères is well-connected by train and bus services. The castle is located within walking distance (around 10 minutes) from the Gruyères train station and is signposted, making it easy to find.

By Car: If you prefer to drive, Gruyères has parking facilities available. However, due to the limited space in the town, it is recommended to arrive early or use public transport during peak tourist seasons.

Accessibility within the Castle: Gruyères Castle has made efforts to improve accessibility for visitors with disabilities. There is a lift available to access the castle's different levels, and wheelchair-friendly paths have been created. However, it's worth noting that due to the historic nature of the castle, some areas may have limited accessibility.

Visitor Experience: Gruyères Castle offers a range of experiences for tourists:

Museum: The castle houses the Museum of Gruyères, which showcases the region's history, art, and culture. The museum exhibits include historical artifacts, furniture, artwork, and interactive displays that provide insights into the castle's past.

Guided Tours: Guided tours are available, providing in-depth information about the castle's history, architecture, and the surrounding region. These tours are offered in multiple languages and are led by knowledgeable guides.

Panoramic Views: From the castle's ramparts, visitors can enjoy panoramic views of the town of Gruyères, the Swiss countryside, and the distant Alps. It offers an opportunity to take memorable photographs and appreciate the beauty of the surroundings.

Castle Gardens: Gruyères Castle has beautiful gardens where visitors can stroll and relax. The gardens feature manicured lawns, flower beds, and scenic viewpoints.

Temporary Exhibitions and Events: The castle hosts temporary exhibitions and cultural events throughout the year, including art exhibitions, concerts, and medieval-themed festivals. These events provide additional entertainment and cultural experiences for visitors.

Nearby Attractions: In addition to visiting Gruyères Castle, visitors can explore other attractions in the area. The town of Gruyères is known for its famous Gruyère cheese, and there are cheese factories where you can learn about the cheese-making process and sample the local specialty. The HR Giger Museum, dedicated to the renowned Swiss artist, is also located in Gruyères..

Zurich Museum of Fine Arts

The Zurich Museum of Fine Arts, known as Kunsthaus Zürich, is a prominent art museum located in Zurich, Switzerland. Here are some details about the Zurich Museum of Fine Arts and its accessibility as a tourist site:

Location: The Zurich Museum of Fine Arts is located in the heart of Zurich, Switzerland's largest city. It is situated on Heimplatz, near the city's renowned shopping street, Bahnhofstrasse.

Collection: The museum houses an extensive collection of artworks from various periods, ranging from the Middle Ages to contemporary art. Its collection includes paintings, sculptures, prints, drawings, and photography. Notable artists represented in the museum's collection include Claude Monet, Vincent van Gogh, Edvard Munch, and Alberto Giacometti.

Accessibility: The Zurich Museum of Fine Arts is accessible for tourists:

By Public Transport: Zurich has a well-developed public transportation system, including trams and buses. The museum is easily accessible by public transport, with several tram and bus stops located nearby.

By Car: If you prefer to drive, there are parking facilities available in the vicinity of the museum. However, parking in central Zurich can be limited and expensive, so it is recommended to use public transport if possible.

Accessibility within the Museum: The museum has made efforts to ensure accessibility for all visitors. It offers wheelchair access to all exhibition spaces and provides elevators and ramps for easy navigation between floors. Wheelchairs are available for loan, and there are accessible restrooms within the museum.

Exhibitions and Facilities: The Zurich Museum of Fine Arts offers various amenities and features to enhance the visitor experience:

Permanent and Temporary Exhibitions: The museum showcases a combination of permanent displays and temporary exhibitions, allowing visitors to explore different aspects of art history and contemporary art.

These exhibitions cover a wide range of artistic styles and periods.

Audio Guides and Guided Tours: Audio guides are available for rent, providing detailed commentary and information about the artworks on display. The museum also offers guided tours in multiple languages, offering insights into the collection and the artists.

Museum Shop: The museum has a shop where visitors can purchase art books, prints, posters, and other art-related items.

Café and Restaurant: There is a café and restaurant within the museum where visitors can relax, enjoy refreshments, or have a meal.

Events and Education Programs: The Zurich Museum of Fine Arts organizes a variety of events, including lectures, workshops, and educational programs for adults, families, and children. These activities provide opportunities for visitors to engage with art in a more interactive and participatory manner.

Surrounding Attractions: The museum is located in close proximity to other attractions in Zurich. Visitors can explore the city's old town, visit other museums and galleries, or enjoy a stroll along Lake Zurich.

Glacier Express

The Glacier Express is a scenic train journey in Switzerland that traverses the stunning landscapes of the Swiss Alps, offering breathtaking views of mountains, valleys, and glaciers. Here are some details about the Glacier Express and its accessibility as a tourist site:

Route: The Glacier Express route stretches for 291 kilometers (181 miles) from Zermatt to St. Moritz. The journey takes around 8 hours, passing through iconic Swiss regions such as the Matterhorn, the Rhine Gorge, and the Oberalp Pass.

Scenic Beauty: The Glacier Express is renowned for its exceptional natural beauty. Throughout the journey, passengers are treated to panoramic views of snow-capped mountains, picturesque valleys, charming alpine villages, and pristine lakes. The train's large windows and glass-domed panoramic cars allow for unobstructed views of the breathtaking landscapes.

Accessibility: The Glacier Express is accessible for tourists:

By Public Transport: The Glacier Express can be accessed by utilizing Switzerland's efficient public transportation network. Major Swiss cities such as Zurich, Geneva, and Basel are well-connected by trains to the starting points of Zermatt and St. Moritz, from where you can board the Glacier Express.

Accessibility on the Train: The Glacier Express trains are equipped with facilities to accommodate passengers with disabilities. There are designated spaces for wheelchair users, accessible restrooms, and staff available to assist passengers with special needs. However, it is advisable to inform the train operator in advance to ensure a smooth and comfortable journey.

Station Accessibility: The starting points of Zermatt and St. Moritz, as well as other stations along the route, generally have accessibility features such as ramps and elevators. However, it's always best to check the specific accessibility information for each station beforehand.

Assistance: If needed, passengers with disabilities or reduced mobility can request assistance at the train stations or directly from the train operator. Staff members are usually available to provide guidance and support.

Comfort and Amenities: The Glacier Express offers a comfortable and enjoyable experience for passengers:

Seating: The train has comfortable seats with ample legroom, and some panoramic cars have larger windows for better views.

Catering: The Glacier Express includes catering services on board, providing passengers with meals, snacks, and beverages. These services often showcase Swiss cuisine, adding to the overall experience.

Audio Guides: Audio guides are available in multiple languages, providing commentary and information about the sights and landmarks along the route.

Booking and Reservations: Due to its popularity, it is recommended to make reservations in advance for the Glacier Express. This ensures a confirmed seat and allows you to plan your journey accordingly. Reservations can be made through the official website or authorized travel agents.

Chapter 3.
The"hidden gems" of
Switzerland

The Verzasca Valley

Located in the Italian-speaking region of Switzerland, the Verzasca Valley is known for its stunning natural beauty. The valley is home to the crystal-clear Verzasca River, picturesque villages, and charming stone bridges. While there are no specific opening and closing times for the valley itself, it is recommended to visit during daylight hours to fully appreciate its beauty.

Lake Ritom

Lake Ritom is a scenic alpine lake situated in the Piora Valley, in the canton of Ticino. It can be reached by a funicular railway, which operates from mid-June to mid-October. The funicular's opening hours typically start around 8 or 9 in the morning and run until late afternoon, with a break for lunch. It's advisable to check the specific timetable for the current season.

The Vincenzo Vela Museum

Located in Ligornetto, near Mendrisio in southern Switzerland, the Vincenzo Vela Museum is dedicated to the works of the Swiss sculptor Vincenzo Vela. The museum's opening hours may vary, but it is typically open from Tuesday to Sunday, from around 10 in the morning until 5 or 6 in the evening.

The Bolle Marshes Nature Reserve

Situated in the canton of Vaud, near the town of Lausanne, the Bolle Marshes Nature Reserve is a protected area known for its diverse flora and fauna. As a natural reserve, it is open all year round and does not have specific opening and closing times. Visitors are encouraged to explore the reserve during daylight hours and follow any rules or regulations in place.

The Museum of Glass Art

Located in the town of Frauenfeld, the Museum of Glass Art showcases a wide range of glass art and historical glassware. The museum's opening hours generally range from Tuesday to Sunday, starting around 10 in the morning and closing in the late afternoon or early evening.

The Lauterbrunnen Valley

The Lauterbrunnen Valley, often referred to as the "Valley of Waterfalls," is a breathtaking alpine valley in the Bernese Oberland region. As a natural attraction, it is accessible at all times. However, some specific sites within the valley, such as waterfalls or cable car services, may have their opening and closing times.

Waldegg Castle

Waldegg Castle is located in Solothurn, a historic town in northern Switzerland. The castle serves as a museum and is open to the public. Its opening hours typically vary throughout the year, but it is generally open from Tuesday to Sunday, starting around 10 in the morning and closing in the late afternoon.

Espace Horloger Museum

Situated in the Jura Mountains, in the town of Le Sentier, the Espace Horloger Museum is dedicated to the art and history of Swiss watchmaking. The museum's opening hours usually range from Tuesday to Sunday, starting around 10 in the morning and closing in the late afternoon or early evening.

Tibetan Bridge Gorge

The Tibetan Bridge Gorge, located in the Ticino region, is a thrilling suspension bridge that offers panoramic views of the surrounding landscape. The bridge and its associated attractions, such as hiking trails and picnic areas, do not have specific opening and closing times. However, it is important to note that the bridge and trails are subject to weather conditions and may be closed during adverse weather or maintenance. It is advisable to check the local tourism website or contact the relevant authorities for the latest information before planning a visit.

Milk Museum, Rhatische Bahn Railway Museum

The Milk Museum and Rhatische Bahn Railway Museum are two separate attractions that are located in different regions of Switzerland. The Milk Museum, located in the Emmental region, showcases the history and production of Swiss milk and dairy products. It is typically open from Tuesday to Sunday, with varying opening hours.

The Rhatische Bahn Railway Museum, on the other hand, is located in the canton of Graubünden and focuses on the history and heritage of the Rhatische Bahn railway network. The museum's opening hours may vary, but it is generally open from Tuesday to Sunday, starting around 10 in the morning and closing in the late afternoon.

Schaffhausen Old Town

Schaffhausen Old Town is a charming and well-preserved medieval town in northern Switzerland. As it is a historic area, there are no specific opening and closing times for the Old Town itself. Visitors can explore the narrow streets, admire the architecture, and visit attractions such as the Munot Fortress or the All Saints' Abbey at their own pace during daylight hours.

Soapstone Museum, Entlebuch Valley

The Soapstone Museum is located in the Entlebuch Valley, known for its natural beauty and UNESCO Biosphere Reserve status. The museum showcases the history and craftsmanship of soapstone carving. The opening hours of the museum can vary, but it is generally open from Tuesday to Sunday, starting around 10 in the morning and closing in the late afternoon.

Cedar Villa Museum of Contemporary Art

The Cedar Villa Museum of Contemporary Art is situated in the village of Bex, near the town of Aigle in western Switzerland. The museum exhibits contemporary artworks and installations. The opening hours may vary, but it is typically open from Tuesday to Sunday, starting around 10 in the morning and closing in the late afternoon or early evening.

Chapter 4
The Transport,Scenic
trains, cabs and buses

Switzerland is known for its efficient and well-connected transportation system, offering a range of options including trains, scenic trains, cabs, and buses.

Transportation in Switzerland is known for its efficiency, reliability, and extensive coverage. It consists of a well-connected network of buses, cabs, and subway lines. Let's explore how each of these modes of transport works and highlight the main attractions you can visit by getting off at specific stops:

Trains:

Switzerland's train network is highly regarded for its punctuality, reliability, and extensive coverage. The Swiss Federal Railways (SBB) operates the majority of train services throughout the country. The trains are known for their cleanliness, comfort, and breathtaking views as they traverse the picturesque Swiss landscapes. Swiss trains are equipped with modern amenities such as power outlets, free Wi-Fi, and dining cars on longer journeys. The frequency of train services is high, making it convenient to travel between major cities, towns, and even remote mountain regions.

Scenic Trains:

Switzerland is renowned for its scenic train routes that provide passengers with unforgettable panoramic views of the Swiss Alps, lakes, and charming villages. Some of the notable scenic train routes include:

1. Glacier Express:

The sGlacier Express is a legendary train journey that spans 290 kilometers from Zermatt to St. Moritz. Here's what you need to know:

- Route: The train passes through picturesque landscapes, including the Swiss Alps, deep valleys, narrow gorges, and charming mountain villages.
- Duration: The journey takes approximately 7.5 hours, making it a full-day excursion.
- Highlights: The Glacier Express crosses 291 bridges and passes through 91 tunnels, including the famous Landwasser Viaduct. The scenery includes majestic mountains, pristine glaciers, and dense forests.
- Reservations: Due to its popularity, reservations are essential, especially during peak tourist seasons. You can reserve specific seats or opt for panoramic carriages with large windows.

2. Bernina Express:

The Bernina Express is a panoramic train route that connects Chur in Switzerland to Tirano in Italy. Here's what you need to know:

- Route: The train passes through the UNESCO World Heritage-listed Rhaetian Railway, offering breathtaking views of the Swiss Alps, dramatic viaducts, and Alpine meadows.
- Duration: The full journey takes around 4 hours.
- Highlights: The route features the Landwasser Viaduct, Brusio Circular Viaduct, and the Bernina Pass. It reaches an elevation of 2,253 meters at the Ospizio Bernina station, offering incredible vistas of snow-capped peaks and pristine lakes.
- Reservations: Reservations are recommended, especially for panoramic carriages. The train operates all year round, and during winter, you can enjoy the scenic winter wonderland.

3. GoldenPass Line:

The GoldenPass Line connects Lucerne to Lake Geneva, passing through Interlaken and Montreux. Here's what you need to know:

- Route: The train traverses central Switzerland's picturesque landscapes, including pristine lakes, rolling hills, and charming Swiss villages.
- Duration: The journey time varies depending on the route you choose, but it typically takes between 4 to 6 hours.
- Highlights: The route features panoramic views of Lake Lucerne, the Brünig Pass, the Bernese Oberland, and the vineyards of the Lavaux

region. It offers a captivating blend of natural beauty and cultural attractions.

- Reservations: While reservations are not mandatory, it is advisable to reserve seats during peak tourist periods, especially if you prefer panoramic carriages.

4. Gotthard Panorama Express:

The Gotthard Panorama Express combines a boat and train journey, taking travelers from Lucerne to Lugano. Here's what you need to know:

- Route: The journey begins with a boat trip across Lake Lucerne, followed by a train ride through the Gotthard Pass, showcasing dramatic landscapes, deep gorges, and charming Swiss towns.
- Duration: The boat journey takes around 2.5 hours, followed by a 2-hour train ride.
- Highlights: The Gotthard Panorama Express offers stunning lake and mountain views, including the iconic Swiss Knife Valley, the Andermatt region, and the Bellinzona Castles.
- Reservations: Reservations are required for both the boat and train sections. Panoramic train carriages provide the best views.

5. Voralpen Express:

The Voralpen Express connects St. Gallen to Lucerne, passing through picturesque countryside and tranquil landscapes. Here's what you need to know:

- Route: The train journey takes you through the rolling hills and scenic landscapes of eastern Switzerland, passing charming towns and rural areas.

- Duration: The full journey takes approximately 2.5 hours.
- Highlights: The Voralpen Express showcases the beauty of Swiss countryside, with views of green meadows, vineyards, and the picturesque Lake Zurich. You'll also pass through the UNESCO Biosphere Reserve of Entlebuch, known for its natural beauty and diverse wildlife.
- Reservations: Reservations are not required for standard seating, but it is advisable to reserve seats during peak travel periods for a more comfortable journey.

Before embarking on a scenic train trip in Switzerland, here are a few essential things to know:

- Timetables: Check the train schedules in advance, as some scenic trains operate on specific timetables and may have limited frequency, especially during off-peak seasons.
- Reservations: For the most popular scenic train routes, such as the Glacier Express and Bernina Express, reservations are highly recommended, especially during peak tourist seasons. Booking in advance ensures you secure a seat and panoramic views.
- Panoramic Carriages: Some scenic trains offer special panoramic carriages with large windows, allowing for an immersive experience. These carriages provide unobstructed views, and reservations are often required for them.
- Seasonal Availability: Some scenic train routes, particularly those in high-altitude areas, may have limited availability during winter months due to weather conditions or maintenance. Check the operating seasons and plan accordingly.
- Luggage: Most scenic trains offer ample space for luggage storage. However, it's advisable to travel

with smaller bags or suitcases that are easy to handle and fit in designated storage areas.

- Tickets and Passes: Consider purchasing a Swiss Travel Pass or Half Fare Card, which can provide discounts or unlimited travel on trains, buses, and boats. These passes can offer cost savings, especially if you plan to explore multiple scenic train routes.

- Photography: Scenic train journeys offer countless opportunities for stunning photography. Ensure your camera or smartphone is fully charged and bring extra memory cards to capture the breathtaking landscapes along the way.

- Comfort and Refreshments: Most scenic trains provide comfortable seating, and some even have dining or snack cars. However, it's advisable to bring water and snacks, especially for longer journeys.

By keeping these aspects in mind and planning ahead, you can make the most of your scenic train trip in Switzerland and enjoy the unparalleled beauty of the Swiss landscapes.

Cabs:

Taxis or cabs are available in Swiss cities and towns. They are easily accessible at designated taxi stands, train stations, or can be booked by phone or through mobile apps. Taxis in Switzerland are typically clean, comfortable, and equipped with meters to ensure fair pricing. However, they can be relatively expensive compared to other modes of public transport. It's worth noting that in some cities like Zurich and Geneva, ride-hailing services like Uber are also available, providing additional options for getting around.

Here's what you need to know about taking a cab in Switzerland:

- Hailing a Cab: You can find taxis at designated taxi stands, outside major transportation hubs like train stations, or book them by phone or through mobile apps. In some cities like Zurich and Geneva, ride-hailing services like Uber are also available, providing additional options for transportation.
- Meters and Pricing: Swiss taxis have meters to calculate the fare based on distance traveled and waiting time. The pricing is generally standardized, and the fares are displayed prominently in the taxi. It's advisable to confirm the approximate fare with the driver before starting the journey.
- Main Attractions: Cabs provide convenient transportation to main attractions in Switzerland. You can ask the driver to take you directly to specific attractions or provide the address.

Some examples of attractions and their corresponding taxi drop-off points include:

- The Matterhorn in Zermatt: Ask the taxi to drop you off at the Matterhorn Glacier Paradise cable car station.
- The Chillon Castle near Montreux: Request to be dropped off at the Chillon Castle entrance.
- The Rhine Falls near Schaffhausen: Ask the cab driver to take you to the designated parking area near the falls.

Buses:

Switzerland has a comprehensive bus network that complements the train system, providing access to areas not covered by trains. Regional and local buses connect cities, towns, and remote regions, including mountainous areas. PostBus is the main bus operator, offering reliable services with comfortable buses equipped with modern amenities. Buses are a convenient mode of transport for exploring smaller towns, villages, and tourist attractions. They often operate on a regular schedule, but it's advisable to check the timetable in advance.

Buses are a common mode of transport in Switzerland, connecting cities, towns, and even remote areas. Here's how the bus system works:

Routes and Timetables: Switzerland has a comprehensive bus network operated by various regional and local transport companies. The routes and timetables are well-planned, ensuring regular and reliable services. You can check the schedules and routes either online, at bus stations, or through mobile apps.

Stops: Buses have designated stops along their routes, clearly marked with signs or shelters. The stops are usually located at regular intervals, making it convenient to board and alight.

Main Attractions: Depending on the city or region you're in, buses can take you to various main attractions. Here are a few examples:

- In Zurich, you can take Bus 161 from Bellevue to reach the Zurich Zoo or Bus 31 to visit the FIFA World Football Museum.
- In Geneva, Bus 8 takes you to the United Nations Office and Bus 5 to the iconic Jet d'Eau.

- In Lucerne, Bus 1 can take you to the famous Chapel Bridge, while Bus 2 connects to the Swiss Museum of Transport.

Trains are the backbone of the transportation network, providing efficient and scenic journeys. Scenic trains allow passengers to experience Switzerland's breathtaking landscapes up close.

Subway Lines:

Switzerland's major cities, such as Zurich and Geneva, have efficient subway systems, providing a convenient way to navigate within urban areas. Here's how subway lines work in Switzerland:

- Routes and Stations: Subway lines, also known as metro or tram systems, have designated routes with multiple stations along the way. The routes and station maps are easily accessible, either online, at stations, or through mobile apps.
- Tickets and Validations: To travel on the subway, you need to purchase tickets from vending machines at the stations or through mobile apps. These tickets are generally valid for a specific duration or number of stops. It's important to validate your ticket at the start of your journey to avoid penalties.
- Main Attractions: Subway lines provide convenient access to many main attractions within Swiss cities. Here are a few examples:

In Zurich, take the tram line 4 or 15 to reach the beautiful Old Town (Altstadt) with its historic buildings and landmarks. Tram line 10 takes you to the trendy Zurich West district, known for its art galleries, restaurants, and nightlife.

In Geneva, the tram line 12 takes you to the International Red Cross and Red Crescent Museum, while tram line 15 connects to the Palais des Nations, the European headquarters of the United Nations.

In Basel, tram line 8 can take you to the famous Basel Minster (Basler Münster) and tram line 11 connects to the Fondation Beyeler, an art museum showcasing modern and contemporary art.

These are just a few examples, and each city has its own set of attractions easily accessible by subway or tram lines. It's recommended to check city-specific transport maps or websites to plan your route and identify the stops closest to your desired attractions.

In summary, Switzerland's transportation system offers a range of options for getting around, including buses, cabs, and subway lines. Buses provide extensive coverage and connect various regions, while cabs offer convenient point-to-point transportation. Subway lines are efficient for navigating within urban areas. By utilizing these modes of transport and knowing the stops to get off at for main attractions, you can easily explore and experience the beauty and cultural offerings of Switzerland.

Chapter 5.
The local culture of Switzerland

Switzerland is known for its rich and diverse local culture, which is deeply rooted in its history, geography, and the traditions of its various regions. Let's explore some aspects of the local culture in Switzerland, including festivals, markets, and sporting events.

Festivals in Switzerland:

a. Fête de l'Escalade (December): This festival takes place in Geneva to commemorate the failed attack on the city by the Duke of Savoy in 1602. Locals dress up in historical costumes, and parades, bonfires, and street performances are held throughout the city.

b. Basel Carnival (February/March): Known as Fasnacht, this carnival is one of the most famous and lively in Switzerland. It features elaborate parades, masked participants, traditional music, and various events.

Basel's Carnival is a UNESCO Intangible Cultural Heritage.

c. Sechseläuten (April): Held in Zurich, this spring festival celebrates the end of winter. The highlight is the burning of the Böögg, a snowman-shaped effigy filled with fireworks. The time it takes for the Böögg's head to explode is believed to predict the weather for the coming summer.

d. Montreux Jazz Festival (July): Located on the shores of Lake Geneva, the Montreux Jazz Festival is one of the world's most renowned music festivals. It features a wide range of musical genres, including jazz, blues, rock, and pop, and attracts international artists and visitors.

e. Lucerne Festival (August/September): Lucerne hosts one of the world's leading classical music festivals. Renowned orchestras, conductors, and soloists perform in various venues across the city, including the famous KKL (Culture and Congress Center Lucerne).

Local Markets in Switzerland:

a. Zurich: The "Zürcher Wochenmarkt" is a large and vibrant market held in the heart of Zurich, near the main train station. It offers a wide variety of fresh produce, local delicacies, handicrafts, and flowers.
b. Bern: The "Bern Market" takes place in the old town of Bern every Tuesday and Saturday. Here, you can find regional products, fruits, vegetables, cheese, meats, and baked goods. It's an excellent place to experience the local flavors.
c. Lausanne: The "Lausanne-Moudon Market" is held in Lausanne every Wednesday and Saturday. It features local produce, cheese, bread, flowers, and more. The market creates a lively atmosphere where locals gather to shop and socialize.

d.   Lucerne: The "Wochenmarkt" in Lucerne takes place every Tuesday and Saturday. It offers a variety of fresh products, including fruits, vegetables, meat, fish, cheese, and baked goods. You can also find crafts and flowers.

Sporting Events in Switzerland:

Switzerland has a strong sporting culture, and attending a local sporting event can be an exciting experience. Here are a few notable events:

a. Skiing and Snowboarding: Switzerland is renowned for its world-class ski resorts. You can attend ski races and snowboarding competitions, such as the FIS Alpine Ski World Cup in Wengen or the Snowboard FIS World Cup in Laax.

b. Swiss Tennis Open (Roger Federer Cup): This professional tennis tournament is held in various Swiss cities, including Basel, Gstaad, and Geneva. It attracts top players from around the world and offers a thrilling atmosphere for tennis enthusiasts.

c. Ice Hockey: Switzerland has a strong ice hockey culture, and attending a game in one of the National League teams' arenas, such as HC Davos or SC Bern, provides an opportunity to immerse yourself in the local sporting spirit. The games are fast-paced, intense, and accompanied by passionate fan support.

d. Cycling Races: Switzerland is known for its picturesque landscapes and challenging terrain, making it a popular destination for cycling enthusiasts. The Tour de Suisse, a prestigious cycling race, attracts world-class cyclists and offers thrilling stages throughout the country.

e. Football (Soccer): Football is widely popular in Switzerland, and attending a Swiss Super League match can be a fantastic way to experience the local sporting culture. FC Basel, Grasshopper Club Zurich, and BSC Young Boys are among the prominent clubs in Switzerland.

These are just a few examples of the local culture in Switzerland, encompassing festivals, markets, and sporting events. It's worth noting that Switzerland has diverse regional cultures, and each canton may have its own unique traditions, festivals, and local events. Exploring these cultural aspects allows you to delve deeper into the vibrant tapestry of Swiss culture and create memorable experiences.

Best tips for avoiding crowds, skipping lines and avoiding tourist traps while traveling in Switzerland

When traveling in Switzerland, you can employ several tips to avoid crowds, skip lines, and steer clear of tourist traps. Here are some of the best practices:

- Plan your trip during the shoulder season: Consider visiting Switzerland during the shoulder seasons, which are the periods just before or after the peak tourist season. This way, you can enjoy better weather, fewer crowds, and potentially find discounted prices on accommodations and attractions.
- Avoid popular tourist destinations during peak hours: Many tourist attractions in Switzerland tend to be busiest during midday. Plan to visit popular sites early in the morning or later in the afternoon to avoid the largest crowds. You'll have a more relaxed experience and better opportunities for great photographs.
- Research and visit off-the-beaten-path destinations: Switzerland offers numerous hidden gems beyond the well-known tourist spots. Explore smaller towns, villages, and

natural landscapes that are not as crowded. You'll discover authentic Swiss culture and stunning scenery while escaping the masses.

- Use skip-the-line tickets and online reservations: For popular attractions that offer skip-the-line tickets or online reservations, take advantage of these options. This can save you valuable time waiting in queues. Research ahead of time and check if your desired attractions provide such services.

- Explore local neighborhoods and markets: Get off the tourist track and explore local neighborhoods and markets. Visit farmers' markets, flea markets, and local shops to experience the authentic Swiss way of life. You'll find unique products, interact with locals, and enjoy a more immersive cultural experience.

- Take advantage of public transportation: Switzerland's public transportation system is efficient and well-connected. Utilize trains, trams, and buses to explore different regions of the country. This allows you to bypass the traffic and parking hassles that often come with driving in popular tourist areas.

- Seek recommendations from locals: Interact with locals and seek their recommendations for lesser-known attractions, dining spots, and activities. They can provide valuable insights into hidden gems and help you avoid overcrowded tourist traps.

- Explore nature and outdoor activities: Switzerland is renowned for its stunning natural landscapes. Venture into the mountains, lakes, and national parks, where you can enjoy hiking, biking, skiing, or other outdoor activities. These areas generally attract fewer tourists, providing you with a serene and awe-inspiring experience.

- Dine at local eateries: Instead of dining at touristy restaurants near popular attractions, seek out local eateries and cafes. This allows you to taste authentic Swiss cuisine, mingle with locals, and often find better value for your money.
- Be flexible with your itinerary: Maintain some flexibility in your schedule to adjust your plans based on the crowd levels. If a particular attraction seems excessively crowded, consider visiting at a different time or switching to an alternative destination.

By incorporating these tips into your travel plans, you can navigate Switzerland with ease, avoid crowds, and discover the true essence of the country while creating memorable and authentic experiences.

Switzerland's best restaurants, clubs and nightlife

Here is a list of some notable restaurants, clubs, and stores in different cities across Switzerland, along with brief descriptions:

Zurich:

Restaurant: Kronenhalle - A legendary Zurich institution known for its classic Swiss dishes, elegant ambiance, and an extensive collection of artwork.

Club: Hive Club - A popular electronic music venue with a vibrant atmosphere and a diverse lineup of local and international DJs.

Store: Bahnhofstrasse - Zurich's renowned shopping street, featuring luxury boutiques, high-end brands, and department stores.

Low-cost restaurants:

a) Hitzberger: Located at multiple locations in Zurich, Hitzberger offers a range of delicious and affordable Swiss dishes, including sandwiches, salads, and hot meals.

b) Mongolian Barbecue: Situated in Zurich's Old Town, Mongolian Barbecue offers an all-you-can-eat buffet where you can create your own stir-fry dishes using a wide selection of fresh ingredients.

Clubs/Pubs/Nightlife:

a) Hive: This underground electronic music club in Zurich is known for its great atmosphere and eclectic DJ lineup, offering a mix of techno, house, and more.

b) Frau Gerolds Garten: A trendy outdoor bar and beer garden, Frau Gerolds Garten is a popular spot to enjoy drinks, live music, and a vibrant social atmosphere.

Geneva:

Restaurant: Café du Soleil - A traditional Swiss brasserie serving authentic local cuisine, including fondue and raclette, in a charming setting.

Club: L'Usine - A multi-purpose cultural center hosting live concerts, DJ nights, theater performances, and art exhibitions.

Store: Rue du Rhône - A prestigious shopping district offering luxury brands, fine jewelry, and Swiss watches.

Low-cost restaurants:

a) Chez Ma Cousine: Located near the Geneva train station, Chez Ma Cousine is a casual eatery famous for its rotisserie chicken and affordable Swiss dishes.

b) Le Relais de l'Entrecôte: Situated in the heart of Geneva, this restaurant specializes in steak frites, offering a set menu at a reasonable price.

Clubs/Pubs/Nightlife:

a) L'Escalier: Known for its cozy atmosphere, L'Escalier is a popular bar in Geneva offering a wide selection of drinks and live music performances.

b) Le Zoo: Located in the Plainpalais district, Le Zoo is a nightclub known for its vibrant energy, playing a mix of electronic, hip-hop, and R&B music.

Basel:

Restaurant: Restaurant Stucki - A Michelin-starred restaurant run by renowned chef Tanja Grandits, offering innovative and refined cuisine in an elegant setting.

Club: Nordstern - A popular club hosting electronic music events and featuring talented DJs in an industrial-style venue.

Store: Freie Strasse - Basel's main shopping street, lined with various fashion boutiques, specialty stores, and department stores.

Low-cost restaurants:

a) Tibits: Tibits is a vegetarian and vegan restaurant in Basel that offers a buffet of fresh and flavorful dishes at affordable prices. They have a wide variety of salads, hot dishes, and desserts.

b) Restaurant Safran Zunft: Situated in a historic building, Restaurant Safran Zunft offers reasonably priced Swiss and Mediterranean cuisine. They are known for their high-quality ingredients and traditional Swiss dishes.

Clubs/Pubs/Nightlife:

a) Bar Rouge: Located on the 31st floor of the Messeturm Basel, Bar Rouge is the highest bar in Basel and offers stunning panoramic views of the city. It features a sophisticated ambiance and a range of cocktails.

b) Heuwaage: Heuwaage is a popular pub in Basel known for its lively atmosphere and extensive drink menu. They often host live music events and have a spacious outdoor seating area.

Bern:

Restaurant: Kornhauskeller - Housed in a historic cellar, this restaurant serves Swiss and international cuisine in a beautiful setting with vaulted ceilings and a romantic atmosphere.

Club: ISC Club - A popular venue for live music, ranging from rock and indie to jazz and electronic, featuring local and international artists.

Store: Kramgasse - Bern's main shopping street in the Old Town, lined with shops offering fashion, Swiss souvenirs, and specialty products.

Low-cost restaurants:

a) Pinte Freihof: Situated in the heart of Bern's Old Town, Pinte Freihof offers traditional Swiss cuisine at affordable prices, including classics like fondue and raclette.

b) Mr. Wongs: This Asian fusion restaurant in Bern offers a variety of tasty dishes at reasonable prices, including sushi, noodles, and stir-fries.

Clubs/Pubs/Nightlife:

a) Turnhalle: Housed in a former gymnasium, Turnhalle is a popular bar and club in Bern that hosts live music performances, DJs, and themed parties.

b) Rondel: Located near Bern's train station, Rondel is a cozy pub known for its wide selection of beers, friendly atmosphere, and occasional live music.

Lucerne:

Restaurant: Wirtshaus Taube - A traditional Swiss tavern serving hearty regional dishes like roesti and sausages, accompanied by local beers and wines.

Club: Penthouse Club - A stylish rooftop lounge and club offering panoramic views of Lake Lucerne, with live music and DJ performances.

Store: Hertensteinstrasse - A charming street in the Old Town with boutique shops, antique stores, and artisanal crafts.

Low-cost restaurants:

a) Stern Luzern: Located in the heart of Lucerne, Stern Luzern offers affordable Swiss cuisine with a focus on seasonal ingredients. They serve hearty dishes such as rösti, schnitzel, and cheese fondue.

b) Rathaus Brauerei: Situated near the town hall, Rathaus Brauerei is a microbrewery and restaurant that serves delicious Swiss and international dishes at reasonable prices. They also offer a variety of craft beers.

Clubs/Pubs/Nightlife:

a) Stiefelknecht: This lively pub in Lucerne features a cozy atmosphere, friendly staff, and a wide selection of drinks. They often have live music performances and karaoke nights.

b) Casineum: Located in the Grand Casino Lucerne, Casineum is a popular nightclub that hosts various events, including live concerts, DJ nights, and themed parties.**Interlaken:**

Restaurant: Hüsi Bierhaus - A cozy and rustic restaurant specializing in Swiss and German cuisine, offering a wide selection of beers and hearty dishes.

Club: Balmer's Herberge - A lively hostel and bar with regular DJ nights, live music, and a vibrant atmosphere, popular among travelers and locals alike.

Store: Höheweg - Interlaken's main street, lined with shops selling Swiss chocolates, watches, outdoor gear, and souvenirs.

Lugano:

Restaurant: Ristorante Galleria Arté al Lago - Located by Lake Lugano, this upscale restaurant serves Mediterranean cuisine with a creative twist, accompanied by stunning lake views.

Club: Seven Lugano - A trendy nightclub with multiple dance floors and a diverse music lineup, offering a mix of genres and a vibrant party atmosphere.

Store: Via Nassa - Lugano's renowned shopping street, featuring designer boutiques, high-end jewelry stores, and Swiss luxury brands.

Low-cost restaurants:

a) Grotto Castagnola: Located in a charming grotto setting, Grotto Castagnola offers traditional Ticinese cuisine at affordable prices. They serve dishes such as polenta, risotto, and grilled meats.

b) Pizzeria Ristorante Molino Lugano: This casual Italian restaurant in Lugano offers a variety of pizzas, pasta dishes, and Italian classics at reasonable prices.

Clubs/Pubs/Nightlife:

a) Madrigal: Madrigal is a popular nightclub in Lugano known for its energetic atmosphere and a mix of music genres, including house, pop, and Latin. It often hosts renowned DJs and live performances.

b) La Cucaracha: La Cucaracha is a lively Latin American bar in Lugano that offers a vibrant ambiance, Latin music, and a wide range of cocktails. It's a great spot for dancing and socializing.

Remember that these recommendations are just a starting point, and each city in Switzerland has its own unique dining, nightlife, and shopping scene to explore. It's always a good idea to explore local recommendations, read reviews, and ask for suggestions from locals to discover hidden gems and make the most of your trip.

List of typical foods and drinks to try on a trip to Switzerland

Switzerland is renowned for its delicious and diverse culinary offerings. When visiting Switzerland, be sure to try these typical foods and drinks that are representative of Swiss cuisine:

- Cheese Fondue: A classic Swiss dish, cheese fondue consists of melted cheese, typically a blend of Gruyère and Emmental, mixed with white wine and garlic. It is served in a communal pot, and diners dip pieces of bread into the melted cheese.

- Raclette: Another popular Swiss cheese dish, raclette involves melting a wheel of raclette cheese and scraping the melted cheese onto boiled potatoes, pickles, onions, and cured meats. It's a hearty and flavorful dish, perfect for cold winter evenings.

- Rösti: Rösti is a Swiss-style grated potato pancake, often served as a side dish. The potatoes are fried until golden and crispy, creating a delicious and satisfying accompaniment to various main courses.

- Zürcher Geschnetzeltes: A specialty from Zurich, Zürcher Geschnetzeltes features sliced veal cooked in a creamy white wine and mushroom sauce. It is typically served with Rösti, creating a comforting and flavorful combination.

- Swiss Chocolate: Switzerland is renowned for its high-quality chocolate. Indulge in a variety of Swiss chocolates, from milk chocolate to dark chocolate and filled chocolates with various flavors, including pralines, truffles, and nougat.

- Swiss Alps Honey: The Swiss Alps are home to a wide variety of floral and herbal plants, resulting in unique and flavorful honey. Try different types of Swiss Alps honey, such as alpine flower honey or forest honey, for a taste of the local flora.

- Swiss Birchermüesli: Birchermüesli is a popular Swiss breakfast dish made with rolled oats, grated apples, nuts, yogurt, and sometimes fresh fruits. It is a nutritious and refreshing way to start your day.

- Swiss Wines: Switzerland has a long tradition of winemaking, and its vineyards produce a range of excellent wines. Try Swiss wines, such as Chasselas (a white wine), Pinot Noir (a red wine), or Dôle (a blended red wine), to savor the unique flavors of Swiss terroir.

- Swiss Beers: Switzerland has a growing craft beer scene, and you can find a variety of local breweries producing quality beers. Sample Swiss beers, including lagers, ales, and specialty brews, to explore the country's emerging beer culture.

- Swiss Pastries: Don't miss out on Swiss pastries, such as the buttery and flaky croissants, pain au chocolat (chocolate-filled pastry), Nusstorte (a nut-filled tart from the Engadine region), and various fruit tarts.

- Swiss Fondue Chinoise: Fondue Chinoise is a Swiss version of the classic Chinese hot pot. Thinly sliced meat, such as beef or chicken, is cooked in a flavorful broth and then dipped in various sauces. It's a popular dish for social gatherings.

- Zopf: Zopf is a traditional Swiss braided bread made with white flour, milk, butter, eggs, and yeast. It has a soft texture and slightly sweet taste, often enjoyed for breakfast or as an accompaniment to meals.

- Berner Platte: This hearty dish originated in Bern and typically includes a variety of smoked and cured meats, such as sausages, bacon, ham, and pork belly, served with sauerkraut and boiled potatoes. It's a feast for meat lovers.

- Älplermagronen: Älplermagronen, also known as Swiss Alpine macaroni, is a comforting dish made with pasta, cheese, cream, and caramelized onions. It is often served with applesauce on the side.

- Swiss Rösti with Egg: A twist on the classic rösti, this version includes a fried egg on top of the crispy grated potatoes. The combination of the creamy yolk with the crunchy potatoes is a delightful treat.

- Swiss Cervelat: Cervelat is a traditional Swiss sausage made from a mix of pork, beef, and bacon, seasoned with herbs and spices. It is often grilled or boiled and served as a popular ingredient in Swiss cuisine.
- Rivella: Rivella is a unique Swiss soft drink made from lactose-free whey. It has a slightly sweet and tangy taste and comes in various flavors, including original, red, and green. It's a refreshing and popular beverage in Switzerland.
- Swiss Herbal Liqueurs: Switzerland is known for producing a range of herbal liqueurs with distinct flavors. Popular choices include Appenzeller Alpenbitter, a bitter herbal liqueur, and Enzian, made from gentian roots.
- Swiss Meringues: Swiss meringues are light and airy confections made with whipped egg whites and sugar. They are often served as a sweet treat on their own or used as a topping for desserts.
- Swiss Alps Herbs and Teas: Take the opportunity to try a variety of teas and herbal infusions made from Swiss alpine herbs. These aromatic and soothing beverages are a delightful way to experience the flavors of the Swiss mountains.

These are just a few examples of the many delightful foods and drinks to try during your trip to Switzerland. Each region in Switzerland has its own specialties and culinary traditions, so be sure to explore local cuisine and savor the flavors of this gastronomic paradise.

Chapter 6.
The Itineraries

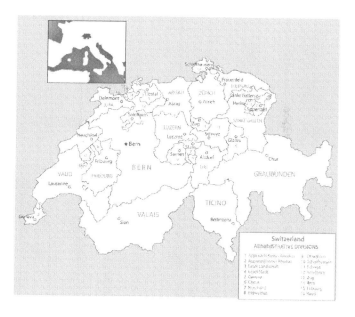

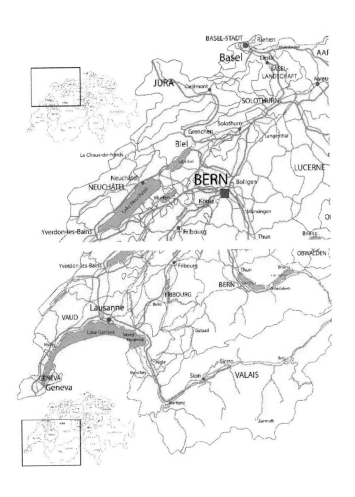

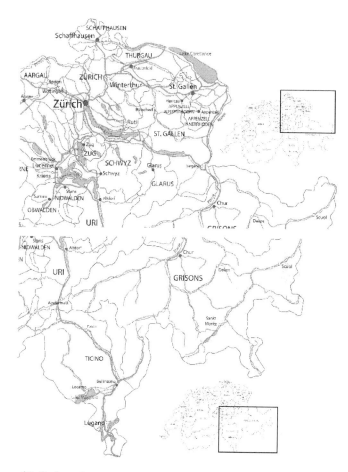

(2-3 days):

Day 1:

Arrive in Zurich: Explore the city's highlights such as the Old Town, Bahnhofstrasse (shopping street), and Grossmünster (a Romanesque-style church).

Visit Kunsthaus Zurich: An art museum housing an impressive collection of modern and contemporary art.

Enjoy dinner at a local restaurant and try Swiss cuisine specialties like fondue or raclette.

Day 2:

Take a day trip to Lucerne: Visit the iconic Chapel Bridge, explore the Old Town, and enjoy the picturesque Lake Lucerne.

Optional: Take a boat trip on Lake Lucerne or visit the Swiss Museum of Transport.

Return to Zurich in the evening and explore the city's vibrant nightlife.

Day 3 (optional):

If you have an extra day, consider visiting the Rhine Falls near Schaffhausen, Europe's largest waterfall.

Alternatively, spend the day exploring Zurich further or taking a leisurely stroll along Lake Zurich.

(6-7 days):

Day 1:

Arrive in Zurich and spend the day exploring the city as described in the weekend trip itinerary.

Day 2:

Travel to Interlaken: Enjoy the scenic train journey and check into your accommodation.

Explore Interlaken: Take a walk along Höheweg, visit the Hohematte Park, and enjoy views of the Jungfrau mountain range.

Optional: Take a funicular or cable car to Harder Kulm for panoramic views of Interlaken.

Day 3:

Excursion to Jungfraujoch: Take the train to Kleine Scheidegg and then ascend to the "Top of Europe" – Jungfraujoch. Enjoy breathtaking views, visit the Ice Palace, and take part in snow activities.

Return to Interlaken and spend the evening at leisure.

Day 4:

Day trip to the Lauterbrunnen Valley: Explore the picturesque valley with its numerous waterfalls, including the famous Staubbach Falls. Take a cable car to Schilthorn for stunning panoramic views.

Optional: Visit Trümmelbach Falls, a series of impressive waterfalls inside the mountain.

Day 5:

Travel to Lucerne: Take a scenic train journey to Lucerne and check into your hotel.

Explore Lucerne: Visit the Chapel Bridge, Lion Monument, and explore the charming Old Town.

Optional: Take a boat trip on Lake Lucerne or visit the Swiss Museum of Transport.

Day 6:

Excursion to Mount Pilatus: Take a boat from Lucerne to Alpnachstad, then a cogwheel train up to Mount Pilatus. Enjoy the panoramic views, take a short hike, and maybe try the summer toboggan run.

Return to Lucerne and spend the evening at leisure.

Day 7:

Return to Zurich: Take a leisurely morning in Lucerne, then travel back to Zurich.

Spend the day exploring any sights you may have missed on the first day or indulge in some shopping.

Depart from Zurich or spend an additional night to relax and explore the city further.

Two Weeks or More:

For a longer trip, you can extend the week-long itinerary by adding more destinations and allowing for additional exploration time in each location. Here are a few suggestions to consider:

Add a visit to Zermatt to experience the Matterhorn and enjoy hiking or skiing.

Day 8-10:

From Lucerne, travel to Zermatt: Take the train to Zermatt, a charming Alpine village famous for the iconic Matterhorn.

Spend a few days in Zermatt: Enjoy hiking or take a cable car to Gornergrat for stunning panoramic views of the surrounding peaks.

Optional: If you visit during the winter season, indulge in skiing or snowboarding on the slopes of Zermatt.

Day 11-13:

Travel to Geneva: Take a train from Zermatt to Geneva, a cosmopolitan city located on the shores of Lake Geneva.

Explore Geneva: Visit the Jet d'Eau, St. Pierre Cathedral, United Nations headquarters, and stroll along the beautiful Lake Geneva promenade.

Take a day trip to nearby attractions like Chillon Castle or Montreux, known for its annual jazz festival and beautiful lakeside setting.

Optional: If you're a fan of watches, visit the Patek Philippe Museum and the International Red Cross and Red Crescent Museum.

Day 14-16:

Head to the Bernese Oberland region: Take a train to the picturesque town of Grindelwald or Lauterbrunnen.

Explore the Bernese Oberland: Enjoy stunning mountain scenery, visit the Trümmelbach Falls, take a cable car to Schilthorn, or go hiking in the region.

Optional: If you're looking for adventure, try paragliding or canyoning in Interlaken.

Day 17-19:

Travel to St. Moritz: Take a scenic train journey to St. Moritz, a luxurious Alpine resort town known for its skiing, spas, and upscale shopping.

Explore St. Moritz: Enjoy outdoor activities like skiing, snowboarding, or ice skating during the winter months.

Visit Lake St. Moritz, take a ride on the Glacier Express, or simply relax and soak in the stunning surroundings.

Day 20-21 (optional):

Return to Zurich or Geneva: Depending on your departure location, you can either travel back to Zurich or Geneva.

Use the remaining time to explore any attractions you may have missed or enjoy some leisurely shopping and dining.

Remember to adjust the itinerary based on your personal preferences, the specific season you're visiting, and any additional destinations you wish to include.

Switzerland offers a wealth of natural beauty, cultural landmarks, and outdoor activities, so take your time to savor each destination and create memorable experiences throughout your trip.

Chapter 7
Accommodations options and Activities to do for free as a family

Switzerland offers a wide range of accommodation options, from budget-friendly stays to luxurious hotels. Here are some tips on the best places to stay in popular cities across Switzerland, including cheaper options, luxury hotels, and even some B&Bs and farmhouses:

Zurich:

Budget-friendly: Hotel Limmathof, Hotel Montana Zürich, Hotel Fly Away

Luxury hotels: The Dolder Grand, Baur Au Lac, Widder Hotel

B&Bs and farmhouses: Zumikon Residence, Bed and Breakfast Casa Almeida

Geneva:

Budget-friendly: Hotel Moderne, Hotel ibis Styles Geneva Gare, Hotel Bernina Geneva

Luxury hotels: Hotel President Wilson - A Luxury Collection Hotel, Le Richemond - Dorchester Collection, Beau-Rivage Geneva

B&Bs and farmhouses: Le Cénacle, Geneva City B&B, La Campagne Genevoise

Lucerne:

Budget-friendly: Hotel Falken, Hotel Des Alpes, Hotel Pickwick

Luxury hotels: Palace Luzern, Grand Hotel National, Art Deco Hotel Montana

B&Bs and farmhouses: Bed & Breakfast Brigitte, B&B Haus im Loch, Schloss-Hotel

Bern:

Budget-friendly: Hotel Schweizerhof Bern & THE SPA, Hotel Metropole, Hotel Savoy Bern

Luxury hotels: Bellevue Palace, Hotel Schweizerhof Bern & THE SPA, The Bristol

B&Bs and farmhouses: B&B Villa Alma, B&B Halen, Gästezimmer am Gurten

Basel:

Budget-friendly: Hotel Rochat, Hotel City Inn Basel, Hotel White Horse

Luxury hotels: Grand Hotel Les Trois Rois, Hotel D - Basel, Hotel Euler

B&Bs and farmhouses: The Passage, Bed and Breakfast at Silvie's, Schloss Binningen

Interlaken:

Budget-friendly: Hotel Bernerhof, Hotel Alphorn, Hotel Blume

Luxury hotels: Victoria-Jungfrau Grand Hotel & Spa, Lindner Grand Hotel Beau Rivage, Hotel Interlaken

B&Bs and farmhouses: B&B Haus Schönstatt, B&B Chalet Oberegg, B&B Historic Downtown

Lausanne:

Budget-friendly: Hotel du Marché, Hotel Crystal, Hotel AlaGare

Luxury hotels: Beau-Rivage Palace, Lausanne Palace, Hotel Royal Savoy

B&Bs and farmhouses: B&B Lausanne Guesthouse, La Maison d'Igor B&B, Le Petit Bouchon B&B

Lugano:

Budget-friendly: Hotel Federale, Hotel Pestalozzi Lugano, Hotel Delfino

Luxury hotels: Villa Principe Leopoldo, Grand Hotel Villa Castagnola, Hotel Splendide Royal

B&Bs and farmhouses: B&B Vallombrosa, B&B Casa Nicoletta, Villa Sassa Hotel Residence & Spa

Zermatt:

Budget-friendly: Hotel Bristol, Hotel Alphubel Zermatt, Hotel Alpenlodge

Luxury hotels: The Omnia, Grand Hotel Zermatterhof, CERVO Mountain Resort

B&Bs and farmhouses: B&B Casa Della Vita, B&B Chalet Annelis, B&B Chalet Valaisia

St. Moritz:

Budget-friendly: Hotel Laudinella, Hotel Stille, Hotel Languard

Luxury hotels: Badrutt's Palace Hotel, Kulm Hotel, Carlton Hotel St. Moritz

B&Bs and farmhouses: B&B Laagers, Chesa Albris Bed and Breakfast, Chesa Quadrella B&B

Neuchâtel:

Budget-friendly: Hotel Beaulac, Hotel de l'Ecluse, Hotel Les Vieux Toits

Luxury hotels: Hotel Palafitte, Hotel Alpes & Lac, Hotel DuPeyrou

B&Bs and farmhouses: B&B Les Tilleuls, B&B Au Vivier, Chambres d'Hôtes La Maison des 5 Temps

Geneva:

Budget-friendly: Hotel Moderne, Hotel ibis Styles Geneva Gare, Hotel Bernina Geneva

Luxury hotels: Hotel President Wilson - A Luxury Collection Hotel, Le Richemond - Dorchester Collection, Beau-Rivage Geneva

B&Bs and farmhouses: Le Cénacle, Geneva City B&B, La Campagne Genevoise

La Chaux-de-Fonds:

Budget-friendly: Hotel Fleur-de-Lys, Hotel Club, Hotel Fleur du Lac

Luxury hotels: Grand Hôtel Les Endroits, Hotel Athmos, Hotel Chez Gilles

B&Bs and farmhouses: B&B Les Nuits Toilées, B&B Villa Beau-Site, La Ferme des Grands-Prés

Fribourg:

Budget-friendly: Hotel Alpha, Hotel Au Parc, Hotel de la Rose

Luxury hotels: Hôtel Restaurant Au Sauvage, Hotel Elite, Hotel Hacienda

B&Bs and farmhouses: B&B Charme en Vie, B&B La Ferme de la Corbière, La Ferme des Fées

Activities

Switzerland offers a plethora of family-friendly activities that you can enjoy for free during your trip. Here are some ideas for activities that are suitable for families with children:

Explore City Parks and Playgrounds:

Many cities in Switzerland have beautiful parks equipped with playgrounds where children can run, play, and have fun. For example, in Zurich, you can visit the Zurichhorn Park, while in Geneva, Parc des Bastions is a great option. These parks often have picnic areas, walking paths, and open spaces for families to enjoy.

Hiking and Nature Walks:

Switzerland is renowned for its stunning landscapes and hiking trails. Take advantage of the country's natural beauty by going on family-friendly hikes or nature walks. Many trails are well-marked and suitable for children. The Lauterbrunnen Valley, the Aletsch Glacier region, and the Swiss National Park are some areas with breathtaking scenery.

Enjoy Lakes and Rivers:

Switzerland is dotted with picturesque lakes and rivers, providing opportunities for family activities. You can have a picnic by the lakeside, enjoy a swim on a hot day, or even try some water sports such as paddleboarding or canoeing. Lake Geneva, Lake Lucerne, and Lake Zurich are popular choices.

Visit Museums on Free Days:

Several museums in Switzerland offer free admission on certain days or times. This can be a great opportunity to engage your children in educational and interactive experiences. The Swiss Museum of Transport in Lucerne, the Swiss Museum of Games in La Tour-de-Peilz, and the Museum of Communication in Bern are just a few examples.

Attend Festivals and Events:

Switzerland hosts various festivals and events throughout the year, many of which are free to attend. These events often include live music, parades, traditional performances, and food stalls. The Montreux Jazz Festival, Fête de l'Escalade in Geneva, and Zurich Street Parade are popular events that offer a lively atmosphere and entertainment for all ages.

Visit Swiss Farms:

Switzerland is known for its scenic countryside and charming farms. Some farms allow visitors to experience farm life and interact with animals without any entrance fee. Children can see cows, goats, and other farm animals up close. Arnensee in the Pays-d'Enhaut region and Kaeserei Marbach in the Emmental region are examples of such farms.

Explore Old Towns and Historic Sites:

Many Swiss towns and cities have well-preserved old town areas with historic buildings, narrow streets, and charming architecture. Take a leisurely stroll through these areas, exploring local shops, markets, and landmarks. The Old Towns of Zurich, Bern, and Lucerne are particularly captivating.

Discover Swiss Waterfalls:

Switzerland boasts numerous breathtaking waterfalls that can be visited free of charge. Rhine Falls near Schaffhausen, Staubbach Falls in Lauterbrunnen, and Trummelbach Falls in the Jungfrau region are all impressive natural wonders that can captivate children and adults alike.

Visit Swiss Castles:

Switzerland is home to several enchanting castles that offer a glimpse into the country's history and provide a great setting for exploration. While some castles may have an entrance fee for certain areas, many of them have free-access grounds and gardens where you can enjoy a leisurely walk. Chillon Castle near Montreux, Thun Castle in Thun, and Gruyères Castle in Gruyères are worth visiting.

Experience Local Markets:

Explore local markets and farmers' markets in Switzerland, where you can soak up the vibrant atmosphere and discover fresh produce, regional specialties, and handicrafts. It's an opportunity to introduce children to different flavors and cultural experiences. The Ouchy Market in Lausanne, the Market Square in Bern, and the Christmas markets during the holiday season are particularly popular.

Enjoy Scenic Train Rides:

Switzerland is renowned for its efficient and scenic train network. While some panoramic train journeys may require a ticket, there are several regular train routes that offer stunning views without any extra cost. For example, the GoldenPass Line between Lucerne and Interlaken, and the train ride from Lucerne to Mount Rigi are visually captivating and enjoyable for the whole family.

Discover Alpine Lakes and Water Activities:

Switzerland is blessed with an abundance of alpine lakes that are perfect for family outings. Explore the shores of Lake Thun, Lake Brienz, or Lake Zug, where you can swim, have a picnic, or simply enjoy the peaceful surroundings. If you have your own equipment, you can also try fishing or kayaking in some lakes.

Attend Cultural Performances:

Keep an eye out for free cultural performances and events happening in Switzerland during your visit. Local communities often organize open-air concerts, street performances, and theater shows, particularly during the summer months. Check event listings in the city you're visiting to see what's on offer during your stay.

Visit Botanical Gardens:

Many Swiss cities have beautiful botanical gardens that offer free admission or have specific days with no entrance fee. These gardens provide a tranquil setting to explore diverse plant species and enjoy a peaceful walk. The Botanical Gardens of Geneva, Zurich, and Bern are renowned for their natural beauty.

Explore Urban Exploration Sites:

Switzerland has some fascinating urban exploration sites that can intrigue older children and teenagers. For example, the abandoned village of Goldau, the old Roman town of Augusta Raurica near Basel, and the remnants of the Bunker Museum in Airolo offer a glimpse into the country's past and can spark curiosity.

Remember to consider the age and interests of your children when planning activities to ensure they have an enjoyable experience. Switzerland offers a wealth of opportunities to create lasting family memories without breaking the bank.

Language

English / German / Italian / French / Romansh

- Hello / Guten Tag / Ciao / Bonjour / Allegra
- Goodbye / Auf Wiedersehen / Arrivederci / Au revoir / Buna notg
- Thank you / Danke / Grazie / Merci / Grazia
- Please / Bitte / Per favore / S'il vous plaît / Pli
- Yes / Ja / Sì / Oui / Gea
- No / Nein / No / Non / Betg
- Excuse me / Entschuldigung / Scusa / Excusez-moi / Dispensi
- I'm sorry / Es tut mir leid / Mi dispiace / Je suis désolé(e) / Dumengi
- Do you speak English? / Sprechen Sie Englisch? / Parli inglese? / Parlez-vous anglais? / Vus chattais englais?
- Where is the bathroom? / Wo ist die Toilette? / Dov'è il bagno? / Où sont les toilettes? / Ussa è il bagno?
- How much does it cost? / Wie viel kostet es? / Quanto costa? / Combien ça coûte? / Quont custa quai?
- Can you help me? / Können Sie mir helfen? / Puoi aiutarmi? / Pouvez-vous m'aider? / Vus po aidar a mei?
- I don't understand / Ich verstehe nicht / Non capisco / Je ne comprends pas / Jo betg capesch
- Cheers! / Prost! / Salute! / Santé! / Viva!
- Excuse me, where is the train station?

Entschuldigung, wo ist der Bahnhof? (German)

Scusi, dov'è la stazione ferroviaria? (Italian)

Excusez-moi, où est la gare? (French)

Dispensi, indau è la staziun da tren? (Romansh)

- Can you recommend a good restaurant?

Können Sie ein gutes Restaurant empfehlen? (German)

Puoi consigliare un buon ristorante? (Italian)

Pouvez-vous recommander un bon restaurant? (French)

Vus pozi recommandar in bun restaurant? (Romansh)

- Where can I find a taxi?

Wo kann ich ein Taxi finden? (German)

Dove posso trovare un taxi? (Italian)

Où puis-je trouver un taxi? (French)

Unde pos jau chattar in taxi? (Romansh)

- I would like to book a hotel room.

Ich möchte ein Hotelzimmer buchen. (German)

Vorrei prenotare una camera d'albergo. (Italian)

Je voudrais réserver une chambre d'hôtel. (French)

Jau vegn resguardar ina camera da l'albergo. (Romansh)

- Could you help me with directions, please?

Könnten Sie mir bitte den Weg erklären? (German)

Potresti aiutarmi con le indicazioni, per favore? (Italian)

Pourriez-vous m'aider avec les indications, s'il vous plaît? (French)

Vus pozi aiutar a mei cun las indicaziuns, per plaschair? (Romansh)

These basic phrases should come in handy during your trip to Switzerland, as they cover common greetings, polite expressions, and essential questions. However, it's worth noting that Switzerland has multiple official languages: German, Italian, French, and Romansh. The language spoken in a particular region of Switzerland will depend on its proximity to these language borders.

Chapter 8
Seasons to travel

Switzerland is a stunning country that offers breathtaking landscapes, charming cities, and a diverse range of outdoor activities throughout the year. The country experiences four distinct seasons: spring, summer, autumn, and winter. Each season has its own unique charm and attractions, making Switzerland a year-round destination for travelers. Let's explore each season in detail:

Spring (March to May):

Spring in Switzerland is a delightful time when the snow begins to melt, and nature awakens with colorful blooms. The temperatures start to rise gradually, ranging from cool to mild, making it ideal for outdoor activities such as hiking, cycling, and exploring the picturesque countryside. Spring is also the season for waterfalls as the snow melts, creating spectacular cascades. The famous Swiss cities like Zurich, Geneva, and Lucerne are less crowded during this time, allowing visitors to enjoy their attractions in a more relaxed atmosphere.

Summer (June to August):

Summer is a vibrant and lively season in Switzerland. The temperatures are pleasantly warm, ranging from mild to hot, depending on the altitude. This is the peak tourist season, as visitors flock to the country to enjoy the lush green landscapes, crystal-clear lakes, and breathtaking mountains. The Swiss Alps offer fantastic opportunities for hiking, mountaineering, and mountain biking. The lakes provide opportunities for swimming, boating, and other water sports. Popular summer destinations include Interlaken, Zermatt, Bernese Oberland, and Lake Geneva.

Autumn (September to November):

Autumn in Switzerland is a magical season when nature transforms into a spectacular display of vibrant colors. The temperatures begin to cool down, and the crowds start to thin out, providing a peaceful and tranquil atmosphere. The countryside is adorned with golden foliage, creating a picturesque setting for hiking and scenic drives. Autumn is also an excellent time to explore Swiss vineyards and indulge in wine tasting. The charming cities, such as Basel and Zurich, host cultural events and festivals during this time.

Winter (December to February):

Winter in Switzerland is a wonderland for snow enthusiasts. The country is renowned for its world-class ski resorts, making it a premier destination for winter sports. The Swiss Alps offer a wide range of activities, including skiing, snowboarding, ice skating, and sledding. Popular winter destinations include Zermatt, St. Moritz, Verbier, and Jungfrau region. The Christmas markets in cities like Zurich and Basel are enchanting, and festive traditions add a magical touch to the winter experience.

It's important to note that Switzerland's weather can vary depending on the region and altitude. Higher mountain areas tend to be colder, while lower-lying regions have milder climates. It's always recommended to check the weather forecast and pack appropriate clothing for each season.

Overall, Switzerland offers a delightful travel experience in every season, with its stunning landscapes, outdoor activities, cultural events, and charming cities. Whether you prefer winter sports, hiking in the mountains, or exploring cities and their cultural heritage, Switzerland has something to offer all year round.

What to pack (also depending on the season in which you will be making the trip)

When packing for a trip to Switzerland, it's essential to consider the season and the specific activities you plan to engage in. Here's a general packing guide based on the seasons:

Spring (March to May):

Layered clothing: Pack lightweight, breathable clothes that you can layer, as the weather can be unpredictable. Include long-sleeved shirts, a light sweater or jacket, and a waterproof outer layer.

Comfortable walking shoes: Opt for sturdy shoes for outdoor activities like hiking or walking in the cities.

Rain gear: An umbrella or a compact raincoat is advisable, as spring can bring occasional showers.

Scarf and hat: It's a good idea to have accessories like a scarf and hat to protect against chilly winds, especially in higher altitudes.

Summer (June to August):

Light and breathable clothing: Pack T-shirts, shorts, skirts, and dresses for warm temperatures during the day.

Sun protection: Don't forget to bring sunglasses, a hat, and sunscreen to shield yourself from the sun's strong rays.

Comfortable walking shoes: Opt for comfortable shoes as you may be walking a lot, whether exploring cities or hiking in the mountains.

Swimwear: If you plan to visit lakes or take advantage of swimming opportunities, pack a swimsuit.

Light jacket or sweater: Evenings in the mountains can get cooler, so having a light jacket or sweater is useful.

Autumn (September to November):

Layered clothing: Pack a mix of short-sleeved and long-sleeved shirts, sweaters, and a medium-weight jacket or coat to accommodate the changing temperatures.

Comfortable shoes: Bring comfortable shoes suitable for walking on uneven surfaces and hiking.

Rain gear: Pack a waterproof jacket or umbrella, as autumn can bring showers.

Scarf and gloves: As temperatures start to cool down, having a scarf and gloves will keep you warm, especially in the higher elevations.

Winter (December to February):

Warm clothing: Pack thermal layers, sweaters, long-sleeved shirts, and thick socks to keep you warm in colder temperatures. Consider thermal underwear for extra insulation.

Winter accessories: Don't forget to pack a warm hat, gloves, and a scarf to protect against the cold winds.

Winter coat or jacket: Bring a heavy-duty winter coat or jacket that can withstand low temperatures and provide insulation.

Waterproof boots: Invest in sturdy waterproof boots with good traction to navigate snowy and icy terrain.

Winter sports gear (if applicable): If you plan to engage in winter sports activities, bring appropriate gear like skiwear, snowboarding equipment, or ice skates.

Regardless of the season, it's wise to pack a travel adapter for electrical outlets, a universal charger, and a good-quality backpack for day trips and hikes. It's also advisable to check the weather forecast for your specific destination in Switzerland closer to your travel date, as weather conditions can vary across regions and altitudes.

Remember to pack versatile clothing items that can be mixed and matched to suit different weather conditions and activities. Layering is key to adapt to the changing temperatures throughout the day.

Chapter 9.
Currency exchange and which foreign ATMs to use in order to avoid excessive fees

When it comes to currency exchange and using foreign ATMs in Switzerland, there are several tips you can follow to avoid excessive fees and minimize the risk of criminal activity. Here are some recommendations:

- Research Exchange Rates: Before your trip, research the current exchange rates between your home currency and the Swiss Franc (CHF). This will give you an idea of the prevailing rates and help you identify whether the rates offered at exchange counters or ATMs are fair.

- Avoid Airport Currency Exchanges: Currency exchange services at airports generally have higher fees and less favorable rates. It's best to avoid exchanging large amounts of money at airports and wait until you reach your destination or find a reputable exchange service in the city.

- Compare Exchange Services: Compare exchange services at banks, currency exchange offices, and reputable online platforms. Look for competitive rates and low or no commission fees. Online platforms often offer more competitive rates than physical exchange offices.

- Use Credit Cards: In Switzerland, credit cards are widely accepted. They offer a convenient and secure way to make payments. Look for credit cards that offer favorable foreign exchange rates and low or no foreign transaction fees. Inform your credit card provider about your travel plans to avoid any unexpected card blocks.

- Notify Your Bank: Before traveling to Switzerland, notify your bank or financial institution about your trip. This will prevent any potential issues with using your cards abroad and reduce the chances of fraudulent activity.

- Choose ATMs Wisely: Use ATMs that are affiliated with major banks in Switzerland, as they usually have lower withdrawal fees compared to standalone or independent ATMs. Look for ATMs that display well-known bank logos. Avoid using ATMs in remote or poorly lit areas, and be cautious of any suspicious-looking devices attached to the ATM.

- Currency Conversion at ATMs: When withdrawing cash from ATMs in Switzerland, choose to be charged in the local currency (CHF) rather than your home currency. This option, known as dynamic currency conversion, can result in unfavorable exchange rates and additional fees.

- Be Vigilant of Skimming Devices: Criminals sometimes install skimming devices on ATMs to capture card details. Inspect the ATM carefully before using it, looking for any loose parts, unusual card slots, or hidden cameras. If something seems suspicious, find another ATM or notify the bank.

- Keep Emergency Cash: It's always a good idea to keep some emergency cash in a safe place, such as a money belt or a hidden pocket. This ensures that you have access to money even if your cards are lost or stolen.

- Utilize Local Payment Apps: In Switzerland, popular payment apps like TWINT are widely used. If you have a compatible smartphone, consider installing and using these apps for seamless and cashless transactions.

Remember, it's crucial to stay vigilant and aware of your surroundings when conducting financial transactions abroad. If you have any concerns about specific ATMs or exchange services, consult with local residents or ask for recommendations from your hotel or accommodations.

Tips

Traveling in Switzerland can be a memorable experience, but it's also known for being a relatively expensive destination. However, with careful planning and some smart choices, you can save both time and money during your trip. Here are some tips to help you make the most of your time and budget while traveling in Switzerland:

- Plan in advance: Planning ahead allows you to take advantage of early bird discounts on flights, accommodations, and attractions. Research the places you want to visit, create an itinerary, and book your accommodations and transportation well in advance to secure the best deals.

- Travel during the shoulder season: Switzerland is a popular destination during the summer and winter seasons, which means higher prices and larger crowds. Consider traveling during the shoulder seasons, such as spring or fall, when prices are lower, and attractions are less crowded. You'll still be able to enjoy pleasant weather and beautiful scenery.

- Explore Swiss Travel Pass options: The Swiss Travel Pass offers unlimited travel on public transportation networks, including trains, buses, boats, and even some mountain railways. Look into different pass options based on the duration of your stay and the areas you plan to visit. Having a travel pass can save you money on individual tickets and provide flexibility.

- Take advantage of free activities: Switzerland offers several free activities and attractions that allow you to experience the country without spending a fortune. For example, exploring charming towns, hiking in the Swiss Alps, visiting public parks, and enjoying the natural beauty of lakes and waterfalls can be enjoyed at no cost.

- Use public transportation: Switzerland has an extensive and efficient public transportation system. Instead of relying on taxis or rental cars, utilize trains, trams, and buses to get around. They are not only cost-effective but also provide scenic views along the way.

- Pack your own food: Eating out in Switzerland can be quite expensive. Consider packing your own snacks and meals, especially for day trips or hikes. You can visit local grocery stores or markets to buy fresh produce, bread, and other essentials. This way, you'll save money and have the freedom to enjoy picnics in picturesque locations.

- Stay in budget accommodations: Switzerland offers a range of accommodation options, from luxury hotels to hostels and guesthouses. If you're on a budget, consider staying in more affordable accommodations like hostels or budget hotels. Additionally, look for accommodations that offer amenities like kitchenettes, as this can help you save money on meals.

- Research discounts and deals: Look for discounts and special offers on attractions, museums, and activities. Many tourist attractions offer reduced prices for students, seniors, or families. Additionally, websites like Groupon or local tourism websites may have deals and promotions that can help you save money on various experiences.

- Avoid unnecessary expenses: Be mindful of your spending and avoid unnecessary expenses. For example, tap water is safe to drink in Switzerland, so there's no need to purchase bottled water. Use public Wi-Fi whenever possible to avoid data charges, and carry a reusable water bottle and a picnic blanket for outdoor dining.

- Seek local advice: Interact with locals or fellow travelers who have visited Switzerland before. They can provide valuable insights, recommend budget-friendly activities, and suggest off-the-beaten-path destinations that are equally rewarding.

By following these tips, you can make your trip to Switzerland more affordable and efficient, allowing you to experience the beauty of the country without breaking the bank.

Conclusion

This travel guide to Switzerland serves as a reliable and comprehensive resource for anyone planning a trip to this captivating country. With its wealth of practical information, expert recommendations, and helpful tips, it simplifies travel arrangements and enhances the overall travel experience.

One of the key strengths of this guide is its practical information. It covers essential details such as currency exchange, transportation options, and local customs. By providing this information upfront, the guide equips travelers with the necessary knowledge to plan their trip effectively and navigate Switzerland with ease.

Furthermore, this travel guide offers expert recommendations on various aspects of traveling in Switzerland. It highlights popular attractions, scenic landscapes, historical sites, and cultural experiences, allowing travelers to discover the country's diverse offerings. Whether you're interested in exploring the majestic Swiss Alps, visiting charming cities like Zurich or Lucerne, or immersing yourself in Swiss traditions and festivals, the guide provides insights that cater to different interests and preferences.

Additionally, the guide shares helpful tips that can further enhance your experience in Switzerland. It may include advice on the best time to visit specific regions, how to avoid tourist crowds, and recommendations for local cuisine and dining experiences. These tips not only save traveler's time and money but also provide valuable insights that can enrich their understanding of Swiss culture and enhance their interactions with locals.

By combining practical information, expert recommendations, and helpful tips, this travel guide serves as a valuable resource for exploring Switzerland. It empowers travelers to make informed decisions, discover lesser-known gems, and make the most of their time in this breathtaking country.

Switzerland's natural beauty, well-preserved cities, and the Swiss reputation for quality and precision make it a unique and worthwhile destination. However, it is important to note that Switzerland can be an expensive country to visit, and weather conditions can be unpredictable, especially in mountainous regions. The guide helps travelers navigate these considerations and provides suggestions for budget-friendly options and appropriate preparations. In conclusion, this comprehensive travel guide to Switzerland simplifies travel arrangements, offers expert recommendations, and provides helpful tips for an unforgettable journey through the Swiss landscapes, cities, and cultural treasures. Whether you're seeking adventure, relaxation, or cultural exploration, this guide equips you with the tools to create lasting memories in this enchanting country.

References:

images: Freepik.com.

The images within this book were chosen using resources from Freepik.com

Made in the USA
Monee, IL
03 July 2023

38620834R00068